The Investor's DNA

Impacting Biomedical Startups Through Venture Capital

Verses Kindler Publication

Verses Kindler Publication.

Website: www.verseskindlerpublication.com

The Investor's DNA
Impacting Biomedical Startups
Through Venture Capital

By: Anand Govindaluri

ISBN: 978-93-49532-11-3

1st Edition

Price: INR 599/$25

Disclaimer

The Investor's DNA - Impacting Biomedical Startups through Venture Capital is authored by Anand Govindaluri. The entirety of this published work comprises the original content of the author, who has undertaken diligent efforts in its editing. The characters depicted herein may be fictitious or inspired by real events; however, they are not intended to cause offense or represent any prejudice against any caste or system. Any similarity to the names of actual individuals, locations, or institutions is purely coincidental and serves the narrative. The author bears sole responsibility for the originality of this work; the publisher assumes no liability thereof.

Dedicated to my parents for their constant support and guidance

CONTENTS

FOREWORD

The Investor's DNA- Impacting Biomedical Startups through Venture Capital

This book was born out as a culmination of the real-life wealth of experiences lived through by my dear friend and an esteemed colleague, **Anand Govindaluri** and that of his colleagues, who have tried, succeeded, sometimes failed, and tried again in the complex world of Pharma and biotech startups. Unlike tech, biotech isn't just about code and speed. It's about science, patience, risk, and regulatory minefields. It's also about solving real, life-altering problems, curing disease, improving quality of life, and sometimes, reshaping entire fields of medicine. In the complex world of trying to be the "First in class" or the "Best in Class", as it always remains a goal that most of the startups are born out of.

But while science often takes centre stage, the business side is just as critical. Especially for entrepreneurs. Knowing when to invest, how to evaluate a team, what signals to trust (and which to ignore), and how to navigate the long timelines of R&D—those are the skills that can turn a risky bet into a valuable venture. Finding an "Unicorn" from a bunch of companies is almost like finding a needle in a haystack.

This book is written for entrepreneurs who aren't just scientists by training, but who are curious, ambitious, and willing to learn what it takes to invest wisely in this space. It's also for scientists or folks with business majors, looking to think more like investors. Sometimes, the goal isn't to oversimplify biotech, but to make it approachable, actionable, and honest.

You won't find hype here. You'll find hard-won, hard learned lessons, frameworks, red flags, and green lights—all grounded in real-world experience. If you're ready to engage with Pharma, biotech not as a lottery ticket, but as a long-term play with strategic upside, you're in the right place.

I've known Anand Govindaluri as someone who doesn't just invest in biomedical startups—he understands them at a fundamental level. His work, his insights, and his ability to spot real potential in a complex, high-stakes field have always stood out. I have known him now for many years, when I first ran into him at the BioAsia Conference 2005 in Hyderabad, India. We grew our friendship; we have met several times in India, in the US, in New York and in Europe for much business and for social reasons. He has also met with my Pfizer & other Pharma colleagues, including those from PreveCeutical Medical from Vancouver, Canada.

This book, *The Investors DNA-Impacting Biomedical Startups through Venture Capital*, reflects that depth. He has, what it takes, especially the kind of judgment that only comes from years in the trenches—backing founders, building companies, and learning what works.

For anyone looking to invest in this space—or even just understand what drives success and failure in biomedical ventures—this book is both a guide and a reality check. Anand offers clarity in a field that's often wrapped in technical jargon and uncertainty.

His experience is compiled into these 200+ pages. It serves as a resource that many may find useful frequently.

Investing in biomedical startups is not just about numbers, valuations, or technology, it's about people. Visionaries, Risk-takers, Builders who see the world not just as it is, but as it could be. Few embody that spirit more fully than Anand Govindaluri, has shown through his own prism with many successful outcomes.

In *The Investors DNA- Impacting Biomedical Startups through Venture Capital,* Anand brings something rare to the table: a fusion of personal journey and professional mastery. From the early influences that shaped his mindset to the hard-earned insights gathered through years of investing across the biomedical landscape, this book reflects not just what he knows—but who he is!

This isn't a cold manual. It's a clear-eyed, experience-driven guide that explains what it *really* takes to back science with capital and conviction. It's for those who want to understand the DNA of a startup *and* the DNA of an investor who knows how to spot resilience, purpose, and long-term value. The word "DNA" in the title of this book is more fitting, as I think. Many years ago, I personally introduced Anand to Dr. James Watson, Nobel Laureate awardee for his invention of Human DNA, at Cold Harbor Laboratories on Long Island, NY. I had a chance to have Dr. Watson come into Pfizer Research HQ in Groton, Connecticut and deliver a Keynote Address in 2003.

Whether you're new to the space of investments or deeply involved in biotech ventures, this book will sharpen your perspective. It offers not just knowledge, but wisdom—and in this field, that difference matters.

Behind every smart investment is a story—and behind every investor, a journey that shaped how they think, choose, and act. In this book, Anand Govindaluri shares not just what he knows, but how he came to know it. That's what makes this book different.

From his early life influences to the turning point during his MBA pursuit, Anand's path into the world of biomedical investing wasn't scripted—it was earned. He took risks, asked tough questions, and built a career by staying curious, grounded, and deeply committed to impact. You can see that mindset in every chapter of this book.

What makes this work so valuable is the combination of personal clarity and professional insight. Anand doesn't just talk about markets, products, or scientific promise—he breaks down what it takes to identify, believe in, and support biomedical innovation from idea to impact. His lessons come not from theory, but from the field.

For entrepreneurs, investors, and anyone looking to make sense of the high-stakes world of biomedical startups, this book is both a guide and a reflection. It reminds us that behind every decision to invest is a human story—shaped by values, vision, and the courage to back bold ideas.

Every investment has a story. In *The Investors DNA- Impacting Biomedical Startups through venture Capital,* Anand Govindaluri tells his—honestly, insightfully, and without filters. This isn't just a book about biotech investing; it's about the mindset and milestones that shape an investor who sees an opportunity where others see risk.

Anand worked with renowned investment company, Temasek Holdings and subsequently with Exploit Technologies, the commercialization arm of A*STAR in Singapore for 11 years where he learned the art of investing, incubation and spin-off management in early-stage as well as late-stage biomedical, pharma and deep-tech companies globally. From his early life influences to a pivotal moment during his investment journey, Anand traces the roots of his thinking and the choices that led him into the world of biomedical innovation. He shares his first steps into biotech investing—not as grand moves, but as thoughtful, calculated leaps into a complex field few understood at the time. Anand has spent time professionally on many continents, with Singapore as a major influence on his career. I have toured with him at Pune, India at TATA Elxsi almost 8 years ago. I saw his enormous enthusiasm in helping youngsters and entrepreneurs, take part and get mentorship from him.

What makes this book stand out is its balance. It's part memoir, part manual. Anand doesn't shy away from the tough parts: the setbacks, the missteps, and the skepticism he faced for backing a sector that many still consider slow, risky, or misunderstood. But in those moments, he found clarity. He learned what separates hype from real science, and what it takes to back companies that aren't just solving business problems—but human ones.

You'll find sharp analysis on the bio-economy boom, the critical factors that drive biotech successes and candid lessons from failures. You'll also see where the future is going, how AI is reshaping healthcare, and what strategic insights matter now more than ever.

Whether you're an investor, founder, policymaker, or someone simply curious about where life science innovation is heading, this book is a grounded, experienced voice in a noisy space. Anand writes with conviction because he's lived every line of it. I worked with Pfizer Inc., in its HQ for Research & Development in Connecticut for over 28 years. I was fortunate to watch & learn how Big Pharma thinks about innovation (Internal & External). External innovation is bought in by Mergers & Acquisitions (M & A) activities where many of the Unicorn startups get acquired once they notice, the proof of concept is completed by the startups.

Read this wonderful book with a highlighter—you'll want to come back to this on as a reference guide.

The rise of Artificial Intelligence (AI) and Machine Learning (ML) is reshaping healthcare R&D at a fundamental level. From accelerating drug discovery to predicting clinical trial outcomes, these technologies are reducing time, cost, and uncertainty, three of the biggest barriers in biotech. For investors, this is a game-changer.

Startups that integrate AI into their platforms are not only innovating faster but also attracting capital more efficiently by de-risking early-stage science. As data becomes a core asset, the ability to analyze and act on it in real time will define the next wave of winners in the biotech space. AI isn't replacing science—it's amplifying it, and smart investors are already leaning in.

The long-term impact of AI and ML on healthcare and biotech investing is not just technological—it's structural. These tools are reshaping how innovation is conceived, validated, and commercialized across the entire value chain of life sciences. In drug discovery, AI is enabling *insilico* modelling of molecular interactions, dramatically shortening the preclinical phase and identifying novel drug candidates with higher precision. In diagnostics, AI-driven platforms are transforming raw health data into predictive insights, enabling earlier interventions and more personalized care. This isn't a marginal shift; it's a redefinition of how medicine is developed and delivered.

For investors, this means the traditional risk-reward model of biotech is evolving. Startups that embed AI into their R&D processes are moving faster, iterating smarter, and making data-driven decisions that reduce attrition rates. As algorithms become more accurate and datasets richer, the capital efficiency of biotech ventures is improving, a critical factor in a historically high-burn, high-uncertainty sector. Over time, AI will enable real-time portfolio management for investors, allowing earlier detection of red flags or validation milestones across multiple assets.

Strategically, AI is also shifting where and how value is captured. Investors must now assess not only the biological innovation but also the computational capability and data strategy of a startup. Companies that own or have privileged access to proprietary datasets will gain long-term defensibility. As healthcare systems increasingly adopt AI tools for clinical decision support, reimbursement modelling, and patient monitoring, the downstream value of AI-driven biotech companies will extend far beyond the lab.

In the coming decade, the convergence of biology and computation will become non-negotiable. Investors who adapt their frameworks to evaluate both domains in tandem—not in silos—will be better positioned to identify transformative companies early. The future of biotech is not just about molecules; it's about models, and those who understand both will lead the next generation of healthcare innovation.

Anand shares his first steps into biotech investing—not as grand moves, but as thoughtful, calculated leaps into a complex field few understood at the time. What makes this book stand out is its balance. It's part memoir, part manual. Anand doesn't shy away from the tough parts: the setbacks, the missteps, and the skepticism he faced for backing a sector that many still consider slow, risky, or misunderstood. But in those moments, he found clarity. He learned what separates hype from real science, and what it takes to back companies that aren't just solving business problems—but human ones.

You'll find sharp analysis on the bio-economy boom, the critical factors that drive biotech success, and candid lessons from failure. You'll also see where the future is going, including a sharp look at how artificial intelligence and machine learning are not just tools, but long-term strategic forces in healthcare and biotech.

AI and ML are fundamentally changing the way medicine is researched, developed, and delivered. From "*in-silico*" drug discovery to predictive diagnostics, they're making R&D faster, smarter, and more capital-efficient. For investors, this evolution means rethinking traditional models. The startups poised to lead the future will be those that combine deep scientific insight with data-driven platforms and proprietary algorithms. As biology and computation converge, the value won't just be in the molecule—it will be in the model. Understanding both will be essential.

Whether you're an investor, founder, regulator, policymaker, or someone simply curious about where life science innovation is heading, this book is a grounded, experienced voice in a noisy space. Anand writes with conviction because he's lived every line of it.

Read it closely. You're not just learning how to invest in biotech, you're learning how to think in a space where science, purpose, and long-term impact meet.

I would like to congratulate Anand, for bringing his life experience through this book to the open table, where many entrepreneurs, readers and students can learn at the outset and take advantage of the knowledge that already resides through real life experience.

All the best!!

Makarand (Mak) Jawadekar, Ph.D.

Former Pfizer R & D Executive, Groton, CT USA

Circa April 16th, 2002.
Makarand (Mak) Jawadekar with Dr James Watson who received Nobel Laureate Prize in 1962 for his discovery of the double helical structure of DNA

INTRODUCTION

Biotechnology is now considered a significant field of interest, providing potential solutions for major chronic diseases that affect society. The COVID-19 pandemic demonstrated that advances in biomedical research can lead to effective solutions during emergencies. Countries worldwide are increasing their R&D innovation as well as commercialisation budgets, focusing on genomics, RNA therapeutics, and digital health technologies, aiming for personalised medicine and improved access to healthcare. Despite the increase in R&D spending, there has not been a corresponding rise in new drug approvals. The reasons are many but mainly attributed to the high rate of failures in developing new chemical entities, lack of funding to complete the drug development cycle, sterile innovation within large organisations and lack of visionary leaders in the ecosystem.

Startup entrepreneurship in the biomedical sector has the potential to address many issues and bridge the gap between academia and industry. Startups play a crucial role not only in building a strong ecosystem but also in creating jobs and fuelling innovation. With calculated risks, some of the founders end up building enterprises with breakthrough innovation that will have a lasting impact on society for years to come. For an investor, the ability to spot the right startup with a scalable business plan is an art- comes from practice! The business of science is not about science alone, but many other intrinsic features such as business model, business planning, fundraising, and most importantly, the integrity of the founders to create value for the shareholders. Founders must also have experience in building financial models and valuing the Intellectual Property, with excellent quantitative and qualitative, strategic and investigative skills. Founders should be self-motivated, detail-oriented, and possess strong communication skills, business acumen, and a solid work ethic.

In *The Investor's DNA-Impacting Biomedical Startups through Venture Capital,* I have tried to narrate my personal journey who dared to take the risk of pursuing a career as a venture capitalist instead of pursuing a career as a scientist. This is a path less traversed by scientists globally. It highlights the importance of risk-taking both personally and professionally. Personally, my mother played an instrumental role in instilling the value of risk-taking ability. Through my MBA programme, I developed strong business skills by learning essential aspects of the field. I have been fortunate to be an early mover in the field of life sciences and biotech venture capital. As a Venture Capitalist, I have worked on several investments across biotech, digital health, medtech and pharmaceutical companies. The book shares a few examples of successful investments and accounts reasons for failures of a company.

The book ends with the future of science focused on Artificial Intelligence (AI) with various applications across the healthcare and biotech industries.

I hope you enjoy reading the book and find it valuable as part of your journey as a biomedical entrepreneur and an investor!

ACKNOWLEDGEMENTS

The thought to write a book has been in my mind for some time; however, it was in mid-2024 when I got motivated to pen my thoughts about my experiences of investing in healthcare and biotechnology companies. The training I received as an investment officer at Temasek Holdings, Singapore holds a special place in my heart and hence it is apt for me to acknowledge all my mentors, peers and colleagues at Temasek Holdings for sharing their knowledge and being a pillar of strength in my wonderful investment journey.

I wish to thank my partners from Govin Capital, Goran Malm and D A Prasanna for their mentorship over the past decade and valuable industry insights. I also wish to thank C P Bothra from Lyrus Life Sciences & Medreich India, Patti White, & Peter Galen from HemexHealth Inc, USA and Gourab Mukherjee from AktivoLabs, Singapore for their insights and contributions to the book.

Special thanks to Dr Makarand Jawadekar, who has patiently taken out time to write the foreword for my book. I thank my friend Srijan Pal Singh, versatile author, CEO, Homi Labs & Kalam Centre, for his timely inputs on shaping the title of the book.

Teaching Master's students at ESCP School of Business in the London Campus has been a valuable experience. I appreciate Medy Sleiman's thoughtful insights on my chapter about the future of biotech investments.

This book would not have been possible without the pivotal mentorship of my Late father, Dr G P Sastry who motivated me to pursue my career in the field of Biotechnology and to my mother, Govindaluri Sakuntala, who taught me the importance of self-belief and confidence as significant attributes for the success of a person.

Guidance from my spiritual teacher, Sri Sathya Sai Baba, who has been my lighthouse of my life and ever guiding force.

I wish to thank my entire team for the design, editing and production with excellence. Special mention to Kritika Kanodia who has motivated me to become an Author and Kasish for being an effective guide in making this book a reality.

There are many more who have made this book possible, and their contributions are humbly acknowledged.

Chapter 1: Early Life and Influences

"Children must be taught how to think, not what to think."

- *Margaret Mead*

In hindsight, I can now fully appreciate the meaning behind these words because this was the foundation of my childhood. I had inspirations around me who taught me how to think the right things and in the right way. I was never limited by one to think only certain things or act in a certain way. And these parts of my life have made me what I am today.

I am Anand Govindaluri, the Founder & CEO of Govin Capital, headquartered in Singapore. My firm invests in early-stage ventures in digital healthcare, medtech and edtech. The core idea that drove me to pen down this book was to share everything that I have learned over the years. I've had trials & errors, made mistakes, met many mentors who steered me the correct way, and eventually come closer to cracking the mystery of successful investment. And that's what I want to help others achieve too.

I was born in Kakinada, a coastal town of Andhra Pradesh, on 14th January, an auspicious day celebrated across India as Makar Sankranthi or Pongal festival. When my father got a job in a pharmaceutical company, we moved to Gujarat. I was given my name by the owners of the house there where we lived as tenants. Anand is a thriving city in Gujarat and is also known as the "Milk capital of India". The name, Anand represents happiness and joy. Since I was a late-born child, I had truly brought a surge of happiness for my parents, and hence the landlords suggested that Anand would be a befitting name for me.

The earliest role models I had in life were my maternal grandparents. They were closely involved in my upbringing. My grandfather, a lawyer, was a strict disciplinarian. As a child I did not comprehend why it was so important for him that I did things in a timely and organized manner. Today, I realize that he left me with invaluable lessons in being punctual and methodical- qualities that have immensely helped me in my professional journey. One of the fondest memories I have is walking with him to a library near our house. We made it a regular practice that not only kept us both fit but ensured that we spent at least some time every day in the enriching company of books.

Our culture has always given importance to a mother who is regarded with high respect, seen as an educator, and appreciated by many. These are the sentiments I feel toward my mother too. She was also quite strict, but only with the goal of making me learn important values like punctuality and responsibility. As children, we do not realize the importance of being in good company. But my mother did, and she always encouraged me to make friends and maintain good relations with those who could inspire me and push me to do better.

And she herself also remained the biggest source of inspiration for me!

Three important qualities that I saw in my mother played a big role in my career.

The first is the ability to take calculated risks. Venture Capital investments, the work that I now do, is all about taking such risks with respect to the technology or the management itself that I put my money on. And I learned this from my mother. In the late 70s, she purchased an apartment in Thane, Mumbai, India, by pledging her own jewellery because my father was against the idea of taking on a large loan. When she eventually sold it in the late 90s, the returns from this transaction enabled us to lead a comfortable life.

The second is the quality of being able to read people properly. In my work, it is imperative for me to be able to gauge the intentions and abilities of the founders in whom I invest.

Third, she was always a woman of her word, and that taught me the importance of carrying through with a commitment I have made. She immensely disliked people who kept swaying from their own word. I made it a point to never do so, and in my chosen career path, it has been a very big asset for me.

Coming to my father, he taught me how to cope with difficulties and rise above them. At one point of my life, I was keen to pursue medicine, but I could not secure a seat. I was very disappointed and felt rather lost. He encouraged me to pursue a course in Microbiology and Biotechnology instead. Biotechnology was an upcoming field back then; if he had not guided me toward it back then, I perhaps would have never found my life's true calling.

In the late 70's, my family moved base to Thane, in Mumbai, and this was a memorable period of my life. My schooling happened there, in a St John's the Baptist High school. My mother's influence made me naturally drift toward the people who could have positive impact on my life, and I found many wonderful friends in school.

We remained a close-knit group for almost 12-15 years. We played, studied, and made many memories together. I learned a lot from them all, and the friendship they offered me will always remain close to my heart. It was in that phase that I first learned how to ride a scooter from my friends there. Though it was far from easy at the start and led to a lot of tumbles and falls, it was a very enjoyable time! My school bench mate, Rangam Bir, was one of my first friends there and still deserves special mention for our lasting friendship.

I earned my Bachelor's degree in Microbiology, Botany & Chemistry from Nizam College, Osmania University in Hyderabad, India. I prepared for the Post-Graduate All India national entrance exam to pursue a Master's in Molecular Biology & Biotechnology. After earning a top rank, I received a full Department of Biotechnology scholarship to attend G B Pant University of Agriculture & Technology at Pantnagar, India.

Armed with all the practical and theoretical learnings that the course offered me, I got the opportunity to work as a Junior Research Fellow.

The project at hand was the Indo-US Vaccine Action Project for Tuberculosis at the prestigious All India Institute of Medical Sciences (AIIMS), New Delhi. The exposure and experience I got during this time opened my eyes to the immense potential of the field that I had chosen. I then made my way to the Jawaharlal Nehru University, New Delhi where I extensively studied and researched about malaria for almost a year.

Soon later, another exceptional opportunity came knocking at my door when I was awarded the *Overseas Post-Graduate Research Scholarship*, a prestigious scholarship from The National University of Singapore, Singapore. I had realized by then that my mother had always been right- the people I surrounded myself with would have a big influence on me, and whether that influence would be good or bad was up to the choices I made. Right from my school, I had been lucky to find good people. My roommate, Dr Dama Ravi Rao, during my days in AIIMS proved to be one such positive influence in my life, for he was the one who opened my eyes to what all was out there in the world. He had visited Singapore for his USMLE exams, and he influenced me to think about it as an option for my further studies and research. It was because of his recommendation and encouragement that I ended up applying for the scholarship, and that became a major turning point of my life.

And so, with limitless possibilities in front of me and excitement about where this new phase of my life would lead me, I left India in October 1997 for Singapore. I completed my second Master of Science degree in Biological Sciences from The National University of Singapore. By now, I was clear about pursuing a career in the business of sciences especially in biotechnology. This is a path less traversed by scientists. I was determined and clear though. I earned my MBA degree from California State University, East Bay, USA. This accomplishment was made possible through sponsorship obtained from Temasek Holdings. Subsequently, in 2017 I was awarded Doctorate degree in Management (Honoris Causa) from Keisie International University, South Korea.

I enjoyed teaching students, especially in areas related to Biomedical Entrepreneurship and Innovation Management. I have been invited to deliver lectures and conduct workshops in several universities globally. My first stint was at Nanyang Technopreneurship Centre, Nanyang Technological University, Singapore in 2012. I have also been giving guest lectures to MBA students of ESA Business School, Beirut & ESCP Business School, Paris, France.

In 2024, I was appointed Professor-of-Entrepreneurship & Innovation at the Sri Sathya Sai Institute of Higher learning, Puttaparthi, Andhra Pradesh, India. During the same period, I was also appointed as Visiting Lecturer, ESCP School of Business, London campus to teach a course in Biopharmaceutical management and Venture Capital to post-graduate students.

The influences I was blessed with, and the education that I worked hard for have been the stepping stones that brought me to the stage of life that I am at today.

NANYANG TECHNOLOGICAL UNIVERSITY

Nanyang Technopreneurship Center

Celebrating our 10 years in Entrepreneurship Education **10**

Reg. No. 200604393R

08th September 2012

LETTER OF APPRECIATION

Mr Anand Govindaluri has successfully conducted two ideas.inc workshops for the undergraduate students of **Nanyang Technopreneurship Centre**, Nanyang Technological University, Singapore and other business professionals. The details of the 2 workshops are as follows:

Business Workshop 1:
Writing an Effective Executive Summary & Business Plan

Business Workshop 2:
Venture Investments, Term-sheet Negotiation & Start-Up Metrics

We received positive feedback from the participants regarding Mr Govindaluri's comprehensive depth of knowledge and effective communication skills for conducting the workshops.

We thank Mr Anand Govindaluri for having rendered his services towards the development of young Singapore startups through the Ideas.inc accelerator program (www.ideasinc.sg).

Regards,

Associate Professor Hooi Den Huan
Director
Nanyang Technorpreneurship Center (NTC)
Nanyang Technological University (NTU)
Singapore

Nanyang Technopreneurship Center
50 Nanyang Drive, 2nd Storey, BorderX Block, Research Techno Plaza, Singapore 637553
Tel: +65 6790 6675 Fax: +65 6792 0467
www.ntu.edu.sg/ntc

ESA

BUSINESS
SCHOOL

September 15, 2023

TO WHOM IT MAY CONCERN

Dear Sirs,

It's my great pleasure to recommend Dr. Anand GOVINDALURI, with whom we've been collaborating in Singapore.

ESA Business School and ESCP Business School organized their international seminar in Singapore in November 2022.

We had the great pleasure and honor to welcome Dr. Anand GOVINDALURI who delivered an enlightening lecture on the Impact Investments in Health and Edtech in Singapore.

His expertise, passion and ability to captivate the audience truly made his presentation a standout moment of the event. His deep understanding of the impact of investments in the fields of health and Edtech was evident as he effortlessly navigated through complex concepts, highlighting key trends, challenges and opportunities in these rapidly evolving subjects.

He also had this smooth ability to connect with our 89 Executive MBA participants from ESA and ESCP, through his passion, genuine enthusiasm, compelling storytelling and real-world examples, leaving our audience with tangible takeaways. He actively engaged with all of them, encouraging questions and fostering an environment of open dialogue. His insights have undoubtedly inspired our EMBA participants, hoping to make a meaningful difference in the world.

Dr. Anand GOVINDALURI, we truly thank you for your involvement and look forward to welcoming you again this year in our 6th edition of our Executive MBA International Seminar in Singapore in November 2023.

Nancy JABBOUR

Nancy JABBOUR

Head of MBA & EMBA Division

École Supérieure des Affaires
Campus de l'ESA, 289 rue Clemenceau, Beyrouth, Liban
B.P. 113-7318, T + 961 1 373 373, F + 961 1 373 374
www.esa.edu.lb

une école gérée par la

CCI PARIS ILE-DE-FRANCE

Chapter 2: The MBA Pursuit & The Turning Point

"An investment in knowledge pays the best interests."

- *Benjamin Franklin*

Since I am a part of the industry that is all about investments and returns, I thought this quote could be the most befitting one to convey my thoughts about education. And I thought it would also help others understand that education truly is like investing in yourself- it's going to help you grow, prosper, and become better in every respect.

Despite the many other profitable investments I've made, my formative years that I spent learning as much as I could about every field that interested me have given me the most successful returns!

I have shared my experiences in studying at some of the best institutes around the world. I got a chance to work alongside some brilliant minds. I was doing the kind of things that any student would dream of.

It felt like my journey had finally found a destination, one where I was happy to be. However, I was unaware of how the journey would change or where it would lead.

As I shared earlier, I believe that a lot of people have positively influenced my life and education. Right from my family, and especially my mother, to some of the colleagues, bosses, and friends that I was lucky to have. Like mentors, they helped me, advised me, and guided me in the right direction. We all need someone like this in our lives.

However, the influence of mentors does not always go this way. I learned this quite late during my education, but I believe it was an extremely important lesson. Sometimes, teachers discourage students from pursuing their ambitions or pursuing a skill that the student believes will be important for his or her future. And because we have such immense respect and faith in our mentors, their word tends to heavily impact our decisions and whatever they say usually becomes a student's final decision too. This same kind of discouragement can come from other channels too, but what matters is how you take it and how much you let it influence you.

Most of my young adulthood had been spent as a researcher. Most of my time was spent in research laboratories working to find solutions for diseases like malaria, cancer, or tuberculosis. As a bench scientist, I was quite content doing the tasks assigned to me like cloning genes, experimenting with mice, and waiting patiently to see and monitor the results of our work. But at some point, I started feeling like there was more to me, and I could do much more than I was at that point.

And so, I thought of getting into the business of life sciences and biotechnology. There was a strong inclination I had developed toward being in the business of science instead of being a scientist. I wanted to go beyond basic sciences and get into applied sciences.

I strongly believed in my ability to commercialize technology from the lab to the market. Additionally, biotechnology was a growing industry and there were not a lot of players in it. I liked the idea that being a venture capitalist in biotechnology would not just give me the opportunities to explore scientific plans, but also business plans, and I could be a part of building strong bio enterprises.

Times have changed now and such a decision would be more widely accepted today. But back then, this was not the case. To get into the business of biotechnology, it was essential to know the nuances of business operations, finance, negotiations, etc. I realized that the decision I had made could not be taken lightly. If I had to take a serious step in that direction, I needed to equip myself with the necessary knowledge and qualifications. Being a science person all my life, I knew nothing of business administration and the various dealings that took place. But I would need to know these things if I had to truly pursue the career that I had thought of.

I decided to take up an MBA in Business Strategy, Economics, and Finance. I felt good about my decision. It would be like venturing into very unfamiliar territory, but I felt excited at the idea of it. However, I didn't quite get this same response from the people that I shared the news with. As I mentioned, the field of biotechnology business itself was not too well known at that time. Furthermore, a highly qualified scientist and researcher throwing away his education and work to take up something so different was unheard of. Academicians were never known to take risks.

My colleagues, peers, and teachers were all shocked at the decision. One of my teachers blatantly told me that he would have never made such a decision for himself. I took in all the things people said, but I never let it get to me. I knew I had to rely on my own judgment, analysis, and understanding to make the final choice.

My mother had always been a role model for me in terms of being brave enough to take risks. She was never spontaneous or hasty in her decisions; but instead, she got all the facts in hand before taking well-thought-out and calculated risks. I think this played a big role in giving me the courage and confidence to take such a big risk at that point in my career.

I had worked very hard to reach the stage where I was, and it was a good place to be. I had no option but to excel in my MBA because the doors of the academic world would be closed for me once I got out of it. It was an added layer of pressure. But I had always, and to date, believe in the concept of Perform or Perish. I knew there was no substitute for hard work, determination, discipline, and staying true to one's vision, and this understanding gave me the fuel to keep chasing my goals.

Furthermore, I just tried to think like my mother in terms of taking that risk. I tried to think about how worried she must have been while putting her jewellery at stake to purchase the flat that everyone had advised her against. And I also tried to think about how fulfilling it must have felt when the flat eventually became our financial lifeline. It inspired me to stay true to myself and brave enough to do what I had dreamed of. I also knew that if I always remained afraid to take risks, I would be holding back.

I was fortunate to get sponsorship from Temasek Holdings, Singapore. Temasek is one of the best platforms to hone new talent. One of my mentors in the organization was very passionate about supporting young talent and I was lucky to be in the right place at the right time to take advantage of this. Not a lot of people were fortunate enough to get it. I worked for Temasek Holdings in Singapore as member of the Life Sciences investment team for 8 wonderful years.

In terms of my own contribution to it, I always knew that how I presented myself was equally, if not more, important than my academic knowledge to create a good impression. I was never afraid to be myself, to openly ask the questions that came to my mind (even if people laughed at me), and I knew that I could rise high even if I fell. That confidence too went a long way toward helping me achieve the things that I have.

And that's how I found myself doing MBA at California State University East Bay, USA and venturing into a new branch of education. It gave me a lot of knowledge about building businesses, and this knowledge was the biggest turning point in my life. The course also had a lot of emphasis on peer study, and I was grateful to be among so many people who were very business-savvy. I learned a lot about the trends of how the biotech industry was expected to grow over the coming years.

My science background, coupled with the exposure I had to the world of business and finance, was a winning combination. It gave me an edge in the competitive world and helped me thrive.

Photo taken at California State University, Hayward, USA upon receiving MBA degree, June 2004

Chapter 3: My Adventure in Investment Endeavours

"Price is what you pay, value is what you get"

- *Warren Buffet*

The financial world is all about commercial ruthlessness. Success in the investment world is measured strictly by three key metrics- Return on Investment (ROI), Internal rate of Return (IRR) and Net Profitability of a business. I joined the venture capital industry in February 2001 and since then have been investing in various biotech, medtech, digital healthcare and deep-tech companies. In 2001, I had little experience in the financial analysis of investments. Coming out of a scientific background, I was good technically in biotechnology and life sciences, but coming into the world of high-stakes investments was a relatively new experience.

I remember how seasoned investment professionals regarded me as an outsider, someone who wouldn't survive the cutthroat environment of finance. Many of them said, either in so many words or through their actions, that I would never make it. That is indeed a tough pill to swallow. But deep down, I knew I had something they didn't- a technical edge in biotech and pharmaceuticals that would eventually become my greatest asset. But to cut it in finance, I had to show that I wasn't just a scientist; I could also execute investment proposals.

I learned, researched, and was influenced by the presence of many great mentors who have helped guide me in so many ways. Interests in biotech and medtech investments were never arbitrary; rather, they seemed to be a calculated move based on the background from which I came. Getting into finance meant learning entirely new skills, understanding new investment tools, and establishing a reputation within an industry that thrives on numbers.

I have always been interested in life science and biotechnology. Even when I entered the finance arena, I already had a very good understanding of the intricacies of biotechnology and pharmaceuticals. I knew how revolutionary these were to change the world with their innovations. I was particularly attracted to biotech companies on cancer therapies and those dealing with infectious diseases; these were monumental challenges, and science was riveting.

However, actual investment requires more than what science-based understanding can provide. In the investment world, a company's potential to solve a global health problem is only one aspect of the equation. The bigger question is if the investment can make money? Can it generate returns for investors? That was where I needed to shift my thinking. Passion for science alone wouldn't be enough. That involved teaching myself to be able to review those companies from a financial perspective.

The scientific advancements were comprehensible to me; however, I soon realized that investments are not closely related to developing a passion for science. Instead, they're trying to figure out if science can translate to business success. The first challenge was learning how to take my scientific expertise and marry it to the requirements of having financial acumen, which I wasn't initially built for.

It wasn't easy going from a world of science into finance. Colleagues who had spent careers solely in finance didn't make matters much easier for me. They challenged me to learn and sometimes doubted that I could succeed on the job or even in this role. There were times when I second-guessed myself too.

But I always believed in the power of learning and that was not one of those cases. So, I thought to myself to go ahead and become as good in finance as I was in science. Therefore, I began dedicating significant time to research, focusing on understanding balance sheets, profit- and-loss statements, and analysing financial reports. I enrolled in an MBA program to hone my financial skills and paid even greater attention to the business side of things. Reading of financial reports became automatic and slowly piecing together how companies work in financial terms. What are the revenue streams? How are costs managed? What is their profit margin and scalability? All those questions were no less important than understanding the technicalities of biotech innovations.

I recall the first time I sat through a financial meeting and understood what everyone was discussing. It was no longer numbers and jargon but the road to the understanding of how investments could lead to returns.

One of the lessons I have learned is that no one succeeds alone. In effect, my journey into investments would have been much tougher without good mentors guiding me through the financial world. I was blessed to have several leading mentors- Prof Chua Nam-Hai, John Nine, D S Brar- they were senior patriarchs in the field of biotechnology and pharmaceuticals respectively. They had watched the biotech sector rise and fall a few times as an investor. They took time off to engage me through the basics of how to evaluate a company from a financial perspective. They taught me that I had to understand science but that just knowing that wasn't enough. I needed to realize how a company's strategic positioning, its ability to generate consistent revenue, and its long- term profitability were factored into each one of those investment decisions. The mentos guidance was invaluable, not only in helping me understand finance but also in showing me how to think strategically.

Mentorship is a way of being put out of your comfort zone. My mentor would require me to attend meetings, network with industry leaders and have more responsibilities. He always reminded me that investments are not about numbers but about people, relationships, and market dynamics as well.

It is because of my mentors, though I began to look at investments on a much larger scale. I moved beyond the potential identification of a good biotech company; there was a need to understand how that company fits in with the bigger scheme of that industry, how it compares with its competitors, and whether it has scaled up to survive in the long run. It really was a great course in bringing me as somebody who technically understands that part of the business to the financial world that made all the difference.

My first year of investment was intense. I wanted to prove myself in the world of finance, but at the same time, I knew that I had to take it step by step. At first, I focused on what I knew best: biotech and medtech companies. Hours were spent researching these companies, working on their financials, and applying for some of the lessons that my mentor gave me.

This paid off by the end of my first year when I invested in two deals- Biovex and Agilix, which was exhilarating. One thing I vividly remember during this period was when one of my colleagues remarked that it usually takes a year or more for a new investment officer to close their first deal. Here, I already closed two deals in the first year. Validation moment for myself and everybody who doubted me!

Early results of positive success gave me the confidence to continue seeking investments in the biotech space. I realized that my background in science didn't limit me but rather helped me as a strength. I could understand the technical details that most investors missed and combine that knowledge with growing financial know-how to help make good investment decisions.

One of the things that came to my rescue was the power to stay motivated, even when the odds were against me. At the initial stage, there were minimal external supports. Most of my professional network doubted my abilities. For many days, I questioned why I left science to enter finance. But there was a hunger inside me that motivated me to go ahead.

Strengths imbued through my cultural background In India, I was always inculcated with the virtues of putting in work, determination, and self-control. All these values helped me stick to what I was doing during difficult times. My background provided me with enough strength and motivation to remain grounded.

It really has been a journey of learning and growing on investing. It was not an easy transition from science to finance but was so rewarding. I realize now that my scientific background provided an edge in that I knew biotech and medtech companies very well. But what really helped me over time was the financial knowledge I learned through research, mentorship, and experience.

Investing is not merely about numbers interpretation but also about seeing more than the bottom line. It is strategic potential, solving real-world problems, and staying financially viable for a very long time. Balancing these two perspectives and incorporating financial considerations have significantly influenced my investment approach. This balance has been instrumental in achieving all my successes.

Reflecting on my initial experiences in finance, I am proud of the progress I have made. What began as an intimidating challenge has evolved into a rewarding career, and I am eager to see the direction my future will take.

Chapter 4: The First Steps in Biotech Investments

"The success stories in biotechnology are mainly due to the straightforward application of design thinking in both the business and science aspects of our lean startups"

- *Ryan Bethencourt*

My biotech investment journey began in 2001. I had just joined the Life Sciences Investments team at Temasek Holdings in Singapore. Temasek Holdings is a global investment company headquartered in Singapore with a 50-year track record of delivering sustainable returns over the long term. Temasek Holdings provided excellent training, interaction with investment leaders, and the opportunity to work with talented peers from Singapore and abroad. As a young investment officer, I was enthusiastic about making an impact using the advances made in genetic engineering and biotechnology. Biotech investments are not for those who are faint-hearted as the risk of failure is relatively high. I, however, felt that this sector was one of the shining stars that could transform the field of medicine and the more I began to learn about it, the more I wanted to pursue that which lies less understood.

Biotechnology, though not new, represents the future of health. In the scientific literature, I found my inroad into the world that increasingly excited me with molecular biology and life sciences. Immunotherapy was gaining prominence in the field amid the extensive data available. It is a very promising idea that the body's immune system could utilize to fight diseases like cancer. This sparked my interest in investing in companies focused on gene therapy, immunotherapy, and T-cell therapy.

Immunotherapy was once considered experimental with limited commercial success. Believing this could be the future, I began seeking startups poised to offer breakthrough treatments.

BioVex: My first initial step was a visit to University College London (UCL) to do a due diligence on BioVex, a startup founded by Professor David Latchman and his post-doctoral scientist, Dr Rob Coffin, from UCL's Virology department. Their work was pioneering in nature, focusing on the use of gene therapy against various types of cancer, but with a special focus on metastatic melanoma and head & neck cancer.

Biovex's lead development program, OncoVEX(GM-CSF), is a novel therapeutic cancer vaccine with both oncolytic and immunomodulatory activities. Biovex believed OncoVEX(GM-CSF) has the potential to offer a breakthrough option in the treatment of many solid tumors with relatively benign side-effects noted to-date. The company has a second development program, ImmunoVEX(HSV2), a vaccine for genital herpes. After thorough research on the company and its scientific data, and spending time with the management team, I was confident in BioVex's innovative approach to cancer treatment.

It was an area relatively new to gene therapy back then and considered still infantile. Most investors shunned it at the time for the long road to commercialization, coupled with the associated risks. Startups like BioVex would be years away from generating revenue as they must go through extensive preclinical and clinical trials before the drug is approved by the regulators and approved for commercial use in the market. Naturally, there was no certainty of success with these kinds of investments, and the failure rate in the biotechnology area was high, so investors were reticent to finance them.

But I was not deterred. In fact, despite the risks, I believed in the potential of BioVex. The science behind their work was strong, and I saw an opportunity to invest early in technology that could have a big impact on cancer treatment. Having done my due diligence, I presented this opportunity to my investment committee.

Getting approval was no easy task. Normally, in such an early stage of the company and with little or no funding, my investment committee was rather prudent. BioVex was seeking to raise £7 million at a pre-money valuation of £10 million. The post-money valuation would be £17 million. It was quite hard to convince the committee to invest in a company where the financials were negative for 4 years, till the time that BioVex would have a partner and subsequently generate revenues. After being rejected twice and having several discussions, further research, and consultations with industry experts, it was decided to proceed with the investment. This was a turning point for me. It was my first biotech investment, and I learned so much about the intricacies of the industry. Biotechnology, particularly gene therapy, demanded a deep insight into science as well as business. Unlike the overnight success one might have for a tech start-up, bringing this all to market took a far longer and riskier road for biotech. A decade would easily pass before bringing a drug into actual use, accompanied by costs running into hundreds of millions of dollars.

BioVex was no exception. Several phases of clinical trials had to be passed: from preclinical (animal) before advancing to humans, followed by three phases in human trials: Phase I for safety evaluation, Phase II for efficacy, and Phase III for further large-scale efficacy, regulatory approval, and eventually public use. Every one of them represented different challenges, and each failure at any of them stood to deliver a fatal blow to the company.

I knew being an early-stage investor brought with it the need for patience. This was a sector, biotech, which took not only money but also a great amount of resilience. And while BioVex's science was disruptive, the road ahead was long and fraught with obstacles.

Three years after receiving investment, BioVex depleted its funds. This is not unusual for biotech companies. Companies can go through millions of dollars of clinical trials and still have no assurance that they will be a success. BioVex's Board of Directors knew that they could not survive unless they had more capital to pursue their clinical trials and keep the company afloat. During this period, the Board of Directors appointed the company's finance director, Philip-Astley Sparke, as Chief Executive Officer. He was assigned the tasks of raising capital from the US and developing a commercialization and exit strategy for the company. Philip succeeded in raising money for the Phase 2 and Phase 3 trials for Biovex from a syndicate of US and European investors. It was a new milestone for the company because, though this step opened new lines for funding, it at the same time placed BioVex on the world map.

BioVex saw its Phase I and Phase II tests move forward after infusing the additional capital. Phase I provided proof of safety for their gene therapy, but Phase II showed enormous potential in treating head and neck cancer. The success of Phase I and Phase II trials caught the attention of potent giants, including Amgen, one of the world's top biotech leaders.

On Jan 24, 2011 Amgen announced its plans to acquire BioVex for $1 billion, including $425 million in cash at closing and $575 million in additional payments upon the achievement of certain regulatory and sales milestones. Following the completion, Biovex will become a wholly owned subsidiary of Amgen. "OncoVex, the lead product of BioVex has demonstrated encouraging anti-tumour activity in clinical studies for the treatment of melanoma and head & neck cancer, and BioVex is currently enrolling patients in pivotal Phase 3 trials in both indications," said Roger M. Perlmutter, M.D., Ph.D., Amgen's Executive Vice President, Research and Development. "Amgen is particularly excited about joining with Biovex and its talented staff to focus on advancing the late-stage investigational therapy, with the hope of bringing it to market within the next few years". It is a unicorn exit from one of the most innovative biotech companies, and that was my first significant success in biotech investing. The credit for this Unicorn exit goes to the team of BioVex and the Board of Directors who collectively worked on this exit.

In retrospect, the assessment of gene therapy and immunotherapy for the treatment of cancer worked well in the case of BioVex. It was a new company; science was new then, and the company was at an early stage with high regulatory hurdles. It was, at least to me a conviction for the science and conviction for the team. It also panned out financially and the satisfaction of having a company working on something that could save lives.

The distinction between biotech and medtech in the investment valuation would create critical differences in how the risk, returns, and exit would be perceived by an investor. Two examples to compare the former with the latter are BioVex, a biotech firm that specializes in gene therapy for cancer, and Sun Biomedical, a medtech firm that specializes in cardiovascular devices. In these two ventures done in 2001-2002, the characteristics given each would distinguish its trajectory and challenges that may go forth.

The first distinction between biotech and medtech is the cost of development. Developing a drug in the biotech space from the laboratory to the market is a costly exercise. It can cost as low as $100 million or more than a billion dollars based on the complexity of the drug and the length of clinical trials. On the other hand, the R&D cost of developing a medical device or technology in the MedTech space is much lower. This disparity also holds function in terms of regulatory, manufacturing processes, and the overall scientific demands of each space.

The gestation period-the time it takes for a product to go from concept to commercialization is another critical difference between biotech and medtech. In the case of companies in biotech, such as BioVex, it takes 10 to 12 years from lab to market. The process is so intricate that it involves rigorous research, multiple phases of clinical trials, and significant regulatory hurdles. Medtech tends to have a shorter development cycle, about six to eight years. In MedTech, the innovation cycle is much smoother, and development and market entry happen faster- especially when there is an overwhelming clinical need or it brings disruption in a space.

The cost of clinical trials also varies drastically between biotech and Medtech. In biotech, clinical trials are generally expensive because there is a huge population base required to test the efficacy and safety of new drug molecules. For instance, MedTech trials tend to be much smaller in size and are much cheaper because medical devices are not always subject to the same scope of testing over large populations. This lower cost structure may make medtech more attractive to an investor who seeks more limited upfront risk.

MedTech companies have advantages in forming partnerships or collaborations when their offerings are disruptive innovations. Large multinational companies that operate in the MedTech space are always on the lookout for breakthrough technologies that can complement their portfolios, and they are more likely to partner with a smaller company earlier in their development cycle. For instance, when Sun Biomedical (renamed as Biosensors International) looked for its first two major partnerships, the company was ready with new cardiovascular stent technology. Ordinarily, biotech companies like BioVex can only draw big partnerships after significant results have been achieved - after Phase II or III clinical trials in most cases. This comes with a higher risk of science, where more robust data is required to show the efficacy of a new drug.

Risk differences also translate into differences in returns on investment. Although both sectors offer good exit opportunities, investments in biotech tend to be much more lucrative given the risks involved in developing a drug. With BioVex, for instance, the eventual return on investment was nearly double that of Sun Biomedical. This pattern holds in the life sciences industry where greater risk very often is rewarded with greater returns, especially if the drug happens to be a drug that proves to be a 'blockbuster' therapy. In MedTech, returns can be considerable but tend to be slightly more modest than the windfalls in successful biotech exits.

Mentorship played a great role in outlining successful investments both in biotech and medtech. During the period of my career, I received intensive mentorship from two excellent mentors: one was a renowned Singaporean biotechnologist named Prof. Chua Nam-Hai, and the other was (Late) John Nine, who served as the former President of Schering-Plough Asia. Here, these mentors drew out invaluable lessons on how to look at a biotech or a medtech company, mainly in the management team and the quality of the board. We looked at the strength of the founders and the management team before moving to an investment opportunity because company leadership is something that is going to carry a company through inevitable development and commercialization challenges.

Equally important is what size problem is being attacked by this company. A more significant problem not only presents a larger market but also increases the chances of success if such a solution works. Intellectual property is also crucial, especially in biotechnology. The better the IP protection is, the harder it is for competitors to enter, which gives the company an absolute edge in the marketplace. While IP is crucial in MedTech, speed to market and the ability to form strategic partnerships may take precedence.

Other important factors that go into the mix are the business model and how you are going to commercialize the product. The plans of a company for launching a lab-to-market product can make or break an investment. Finally, the exit strategy, as well as probable returns on investment are always in the mind of an investor. Most investment decisions are driven by the prospects of returns, including when they are likely to arrive along with chances of attractive exits.

However, what separates great investors from mediocre ones is not just technical know-how but also softer qualities like discipline, integrity, and the capacity to divine the trend of what lies ahead. Good investors are not just responsive; they can sense trends in markets and technologies. This allowed me, particularly in the case of

BioVex and Sun Biomedical, to anticipate the future development of gene therapy and cardiovascular technology, allowing investments early on that proved to be blockbusters and exit rich.

The value of mentorship, prediction, and deep knowledge of the industry cannot be ignored. My mentors were veterans of great experience, having witnessed the evolution of over four decades of the biotech and medtech industries. Using their experience, wisdom, and insights, I refined my approach to investment with informed decisions that not only relied on data but also on intuition and foresight.

In conclusion, both biotech and medtech are interesting investments. Investments in these two are generally ripe and costlier but offer higher returns on investments to those willing to take the challenge. Medtech, on the other hand, offers a more predictable path to exit since its development cycles are shorter and costs are lower, though the returns may not be as astronomical. Meanwhile, the real success story is someone who can make successful investments in either sector, and this presupposes having a good understanding of science, a disciplined approach to evaluation, and seeing before others the potential for future success - way before it becomes so obvious that anyone with a good instinct would buy it.

Chapter 5: Understanding the Bioeconomy Boom

"Green isn't always sustainable; Governments have the choice to use the bioeconomy as a source of regenerative and sustainable development that upholds the rights of citizens and protects crucial ecological systems"

- *Patrick Schroder, Chatam House London*

Bioeconomy focuses on the use of biological resources, such as plants and animals, microorganisms, and bio-based materials, to produce goods and services and even energy. What makes this approach revolutionary is how it integrates nature into the heart of economic activity. From `bioplastics and biodegradable clothing to bio-based energy, be it biomass power that one day could change the way we live and the way we sustain our planet.

For me, the bioeconomy is a new paradigm in thinking about production: no more wasting finite resources but through biology, renewable, and sustainable processes. It's exciting because we're moving toward a circular economy where everything reduces waste, recycles biological materials, and creates new opportunities for growth with the protection of the environment. Bioenergy is a good example of an energy source that comes from organic matter.

Reducing reliance on fossil fuels has shown not only energy security but also jobs in the agriculture and manufacturing sectors.

What is more striking, however, is the tremendous expansion of the bioeconomy. It is no longer an agriculture or energy game, although these are indeed large markets. Now, almost every sector—from manufacturing and construction to professional services—is adopting bio-based inputs like crops and microorganisms. It is surprising to see how industries are capitalizing on the advances of biotechnology for the development of sustainable products. For instance, think of developing biodegradable plastics or even intelligent proteins that could replace normal means of food sources while simultaneously causing minimal damage to the environment.

India has made significant advances in the Bioeconomy over the past decade. In 2024, the Indian Union Cabinet approved the *Bio E3* policy, an abbreviation for *Biotechnology for Economy, Environment, and Employment.* The policy marks a landmark move to encourage high-performance biomanufacturing and innovation in bio-based industries; it is a clear vision for setting up bio-manufacturing hubs across India where startups and industry partners will collaborate in developing specialized chemicals, smart proteins, enzymes, and functional foods. Not only are these hubs fostering economic growth, but they also help with national priorities such as sustainability and climate resilience.

I find one of the most exciting aspects about the policy of Bio E3 is its emphasis on *innovation*. Innovation-led BioE3 policy helps create new jobs, boost production in the economy and push boundaries towards what is possible in biotechnology. Bio E3 policy, which is supported through research and development in climate-resilient agriculture, precision biotherapeutics, and carbon capture, is positioning India at the very forefront of bio-based production worldwide. The policy also encourages the establishment of bio-artificial intelligence hubs and bio-foundries that will provide the best of biotechnology combined with leading-edge AI technologies. It is a forward-thinking approach that feel as if the future has already started arriving.

It's refreshing to hear more people talk about the bioeconomy. More people are now finally recognizing that this type of economic growth, the one that feeds off finite resources like fossil fuels, can't continue. We find all around us that the effects of climate change demand a new paradigm of stewardship and sustainability. This is the bioeconomy: using science to manage our planet's renewable biological resources in ways supportive of a circular, low-carbon economy.

Imagine crops, forests, aquaculture, livestock, and microorganisms formed into a highly efficient, sustainable system that will feed, provide raw materials, and even generate the energy needed by humans - without using the world's resources. Not just an environmental question but also a productivity issue. We can create closed-loop operations where all things are in use, reused, recycled, or returned to nature without causing waste, using new technologies and bio-based processes. That is the kind of innovation that makes me hopeful about the future.

In a nutshell, the bioeconomy is one of the few alternative ways forward. It is a vision towards more environmentally friendly world. Thereby, economic development and environmental protection are not to be worse off because of each other. Every time I read something new about this emerging industry, I remain upbeat. We are at a crossroads, and the bioeconomy is one of those opportunities in life that allow for the real balance between our economic interests and the extreme urgency of protecting this planet for our future generations.

Thinking of the evolution of the bioeconomy, my word is innovation. The mechanistic ecosystem of production and automation using nature's resources is a powerful theme for the bioeconomy, and the emergence of biofoundries and biomanufacturing within it will hint at the beginning of a new avenue for growth.

For example, this can be clearly seen in Asia through such organizations as Royal Golden Eagle (RGE), a Singaporean-headquartered resources and manufacturing group that has been gaining headlines for upholding sustainability. Since its foundation more than 50 years ago, RGE has consistently stayed focused on forestry, plantations, and agriculture. Most impressive, though, is how their products have found their way into our daily lives—paper, tissues, clothing made from viscose fibres, and even palm oil for cooking. It is indeed quite difficult not to imagine a world that doesn't rely on those products, but one is even more fascinated by how RGE drives innovation through renewable solutions.

RGE employs around 70,000 people and has total assets worth over US$35 billion. This company is further growing operations under renewable solutions and conservation efforts in China, Brazil, Canada, and Spain as a contribution to the improvement of life quality for local communities. To my mind, this is how the bioeconomy seamlessly mingles technological advancement with a deep respect for the environment.

Indonesia, especially the island of Sumatra, is sitting at the cutting edge of the change. Sumatra has started to become the innovation centre for RGE: initiatives are set to reduce their carbon footprint to the minimum and ensure that their operations are as sustainable as can be. Renewable energy sources in the form of solar and biomass are just the start; they will also seek to apply the latest technology in tracking seedlings and develop new agriculture based on the use of drones. The high-tech approach is not about the highest yields but more an effort to establish a sustainable relationship with nature. The main step taken is the adoption of a high conservation value policy, whereby both biological and ecological values that would attach to ecological, social, and cultural values of the land they manage can be considered, thus enabling them to maintain a balance between production and conservation. With the development of sustainably managed plantations, RGE creates a buffer area that protects conservation and restoration areas on its holdings by employing an innovative approach to continue harvesting valuable resources while giving importance to environmental stewardship.

Biofoundries are platforms that accelerate experimentation and development of products where researchers design, build, test, and refine bioproducts within a streamlined workflow. I believe biofoundries are a giant leap ahead of what humanity can make biotechnological innovations available to. Highly modular, the facility catapults product development and innovation processes into spheres they couldn't previously reach. Imagine a space where a variety of different research teams collaborate and exchange ideas over processes in an atmosphere free from many common barriers often found in R&D environments. Such an atmosphere nurtures an environment of creativity and scientific inquiry. The biofoundry concept assumes much significance in the context of India's Bio E3 policy, which focuses on biomanufacturing and targets the establishment of biofoundries across the country.

Therefore, yet another important focus of work in the contemporary notion of a foundry will be to unlock the potential of parts of genome sequences that are not being expressed. For example, pathway reconstruction based on deep learning algorithms can create enzymes and metabolites that were previously hard to produce. Such fine manipulative powers over biological systems could translate to breakthroughs in biobased chemicals, and functional foods, among other sustainable products.

The future for biofoundries lies in integrating them into global alliances. The international collaborations and best practices shared through the Global Biofoundries Alliance will further increase the global reach of the biofoundries. Being part of such consortia, for instance, Genome Project does not just plunge one's knowledge further but pushes innovation forward at incredible speed.

But when I see the future of the bioeconomy landscape and its prospects, I believe that the role of a foundry will unleash innovation. Biofoundry is not a biolab but an *innovation hub* that could change the face of industries. Having functional genomics at its core and linking with artificial intelligence, biofoundries will streamline the processes of biomanufacturing to be more efficient and productive.

I quite recently stumbled across the development of an automated recommendation tool to assist biologists in engineering biological systems. This type of technology represents how AI can work to improve the efficiency of biological engineering to iterate quicker and produce better results. The relationship between AI and biofoundries is a great harbinger of things to come.

The Bio E3 of India has established a robust infrastructure of biomanufacturing and biotechnological research. With thematic sectors such as high-value biobased chemicals, biopolymers, precision biotherapeutics, and climate-resilient agriculture, this policy attempts to bring sustainable and innovative answers to global challenges.

Under the Indian government, this policy seeks innovation-driven support towards research and development, entrepreneurship, and technological advancements. It looks to establish bio-AI hubs as well as biofoundries for cutting-edge biotechnological research incubators. With the country's biodiversity and an ever-growing burgeoning technology sector, the challenges to overcome are indeed limitless.

This policy undertaken by the Department of Biotechnology in India will increase the commitment toward a more advanced and sustainable bioeconomy. Thus, India is forging its position into the global landscape of the bioeconomy by collaborating with industry partners, startups, and research institutions.

I am excited to see how tomorrow will be for the bioeconomy. It is only now that we are really at the beginning of the innovations that we see every day. And with the setting up of biofoundries, fast advances in artificial intelligence and the ever-increasing influence of sustainability now seems to well fall in place to have an era where both economic growth and environmental preservation are accorded first place.

The bioeconomy is much more than a concept on paper; it is moving the tide in business, revolutionizing sectors, and opening opportunities for growth.

As people in society, there is an obligation to encourage, foster, and sustain initiatives that will ensure the continued growth of the bioeconomy for generations to come by embracing biomanufacturing and taking advantage of the potential offered by a foundry. The journey has just started, and I am excited to see where it takes us.

This is the reason why there is utmost importance attached to taking an interest in digging deeper into the potential of the bioeconomy. Some significant aspects of the same, including artificial intelligence (AI), efficiency, and innovation, are being explored these days with the help of predictive tools in pathway reconstruction. In this domain, AI has remained as a support but is expected to be the actual hero that will dictate the economy of nations, especially the biotechnology sector.

I am excited about the revolution of biotechnology by AI, for example, the analysis of huge datasets that reveal patterns in those datasets-in short, it changes completely our understanding of biological systems, as it allows for the detail that is required when designing and developing bioprocesses using industrially established hosts, such as bacteria, yeast, and mammalian cells. The aim is to modify hosts at the genetic level in a way that could make them more favourable for the optimization of bioprocesses and lead to an increase in the flux of commercially relevant biomolecules produced. Imagine how this could impact fields from pharmaceuticals to food production, where the potential to produce quality products at scale is dramatically reduced in price and readily available in much greater quantities.

However, biomanufacturing optimization is a very challenging path. One of the challenges comes from overexpression of recombinant proteins. To overexpress the target proteins on a large scale, host cells are engineered to such an extent that delivering large amounts of excess proteins becomes challenging and often poses severe metabolic burdens on these cells. Cells responding to such severe stress often institute cellular mechanisms that downregulate the target protein; this, in turn, stimulates overall productivity.

This paradox sets forth the fine balance that needs to be attained in biomanufacturing processes. It is here that AI insights are priceless; researchers model metabolic pathways, predict how these changes impact the overall cell's health, and base decisions on gene editing as well as bioprocess design accordingly. This prognostic capacity is crucial in keeping us away from the pitfalls of metabolic overload and ensuring that our engineered hosts continue viable and productive.

Former CEO of Google Eric Smith proved very bold last year by stating that in the next decade, the bioeconomy might be worth a whopping $4 trillion. His team is reportedly working hard to exploit this potential, and it's clear how many entrepreneurs and scientists are the same dreamers. One powerful duo has been frantically developing the concept of biotechnology for five years. Headquartered in Singapore, AlloZions has been at the forefront of innovation in winning the Future Food Asia award in recognition of pioneering startups in the agri-food space. Born at an important moment in the biotechnology landscape in 2017, AlloZions stood ready to take on the 21st century, preparing to transform and create its legacy on Earth. Dr Payman Saleh was doing his PhD at the National University of Singapore, and his co-founder, Dr Akbar Vaidhi, a serial entrepreneur, was already deep in idea generation for new ventures, so they both saw massive potential for the use of enzymes as indispensable molecules-catalysers of biochemical reactions. These are essentially proteins that enable reactions by amplifying yields and efficiencies in each process. While they require certain conditions to grow, it is in the discovery and development of such products that they pose a challenging but essential task.

Allozion is equipped with advanced data analytics and biology knowledge, the company is building a next-generation synthetic biology platform that leverages ultra-high-throughput microfluidics. This innovation allows for speedy experimentation and optimization of enzyme properties to realize breakthroughs in many fields of production, biofuels, and pharmaceuticals to name a few. Its story of growth, from university spin-out to emerging market leader, embodies all the possibilities that go along with biotechnology plus collaboration and innovation.

The principles guiding the founders of AlloZions make for a remarkable lesson to entrepreneurs who aspire to partake in the bioeconomy. First, they emphasize addressing a big problem in a growing sector. This principle comes first; passion fuels innovation and strives over the intricacies of entrepreneurial pursuits. They also advocate for miracles of thinking big, urging aspiring innovators to think high and contemplate transforming solutions. Becoming the "Google of enzymes" is the very ideal mindset.

Another critical principle is to be at the right place at the right time. The current climate about the investment and interest in the different areas of biotechnology provides opportunities for breakthroughs. The last principle must be a winning team with a global mindset from day one. For a dynamic field like biotechnology, working with diverse expertise helps provide the much-needed innovation momentum.

While envisioning the future of bioeconomy, there is a deep ingrained relationship between nature and overall economic prosperity. The services of nature give rise to a substantial portion of the world's GDP, more than half of $44 trillion. These statistics underscore why our natural resources need to be protected. Absence of a strong national policy as well as company policy that would foster the protection of biodiversity, businesses are likely to be adversely impacted by disruptions in operations and supply chains - and these impacts are likely to spread further throughout the economy as a whole.

Valuing and protecting natural capital is, therefore, more important in the ASEAN region where biodiversity is incredibly rich. Sustainability would mean building a resilient and sustainable bioeconomy for everyone. The bioeconomy can transform biological resources from land and sea into the essential goods that serve billions of people daily. This part of the world, ASEAN, has such immense variability in ecosystems and cultural heritage, and it is deeply poised to lead the game in this transformative movement.

It will be accomplished with the creation and execution of very resilient policies that encourage investment in biodiversity protection and sustainable practices. Governments and businesses must be aware of the financial benefits of healthy ecosystems and their services. Cultivating a culture of sustainability and innovation will ensure that the ASEAN area can cultivate a strong bioeconomy that promotes livelihoods while preserving its natural heritage.

AI-based biomanufacturing and innovative work emerging from companies like AlloZions prove the potential that the bioeconomy embodies, and how it can navigate complex issues in this new landscape without losing principles guiding us toward a brighter future: collaboration, innovation, and sustainability.

Reflecting on the journey ahead, I'm very optimistic about what the role of biotechnology means for our economy and our environment. Intersected with AI, there are likely to be potential revolutions in industries, improvements in efficiencies, and viable solutions to our most precipitous challenges. We shall value our natural capital and tap into the power of innovation, forging resiliency and prosperity for a bioeconomy. And that shall sustain not only today but future generations.

Therefore, one can claim that the bright future of the bioeconomy is marked by opportunities for growth and innovation as well as for sustainability. As has happened in human history, it is a new time for progress-industrial maturity, coupled with outstandingly influential achievements created by visionary companies promising a boom of progress through AI-boosted biomanufacturing. We can unlock the full potential of the bioeconomy with these advancements and our commitment to our natural resources, promising all a bright and thriving future.

As I go deeper into the tapestry of the bioeconomy, I am quite astounded how regions which occupy only 3% of this planet contain a great portion of the known plant and animal species, with ASEAN countries taking almost one-fifth of this treasure. Such unique biodiversity poses both opportunities and challenges to the developing economies of ASEAN. This region holds great promise to contribute significantly more to the global bioeconomy, which presently employs over 8% of the workforce and generates an impressive $2.3 trillion annually. With forecasts indicating further augmentations, I am led to ask how ASEAN can tap into these prospects in tandem with the pressing challenge of biodiversity loss.

Habitat destruction, introduction of invasive species, climate change, and pollution all loom large over the bioeconomy of ASEAN. Can the ASEAN bioeconomy grow sizably while concurrently mitigating the risks or is this an important question we must tackle upfront? This balance between economic growth and environmental stewardship will not only determine the future course of the regional economy but also the health of ecosystems in the region.

And so let me take a moment to step back and reflect on the larger landscape of the global bioeconomy. If we consider just the United States market, the bioeconomy-agricultural biotechnology, bio-based products, and substitutes for petroleum stretch out over a staggering $950 billion. That's a significant figure, to be sure, but it also creates an image of opportunity: changing an industry, spurring economic growth through biotechnology, with great potential comes a great deal of responsibility. So, therefore, developing the bioeconomy must take a keen sense of awareness about its impacts on biodiversity and the environment.

Bio-manufacturing is one area that covers all aspects of business management. There are security concerns in the supply chain, sustainability, impacts on the environment, workflow efficiency, workforce dynamics, and generation of new technologies and materials, among many others. So, going through all these dynamics, I came to realize that the production sector of drugs comprises the main part of the biotechnology industry. This makes strategic assertions necessary so our technological advances in this area do not jeopardize ecological health.

It is in this that organizations like BioMADE find their purpose. BioMADE is named after the acronym: *Bio-Industrial Manufacturing Innovation Institute,* and the institute was founded by Doug Friedman, who is also the CEO. His role as a strategic adviser to the White House Office of Science and Technology Policy makes his work with BioMADE even more relevant to the development of the bioeconomy in the future. The institute is working towards helping the United States ensure and establish a strong position for itself in the production of chemicals, materials, and other products that are not health-care products, through biology and biological systems.

Analyzing the purpose of BioMADE inspires me with its commitment towards integrating sustainability into the manufacturing process. They emphasize the heavy usage of biological systems for producing commodities that meet market demand while doing the least harm to the environment. In this sense, this focus on economic growth in tandem with ecological responsibility could guide ASEAN in further developing its bioeconomy.

Cooperation among the ASEAN government, businesses, and research institutions is a key component of a sustainable bioeconomy. A cohesive ecosystem with an emphasis on innovation and sustainability challenges biodiversity loss while making a huge contribution to economic development. ASEAN governments should advance policies toward environment-friendly practices and investment in biodiversity. This would come in the form of research and development drives or incentives to companies that undertake environmentally friendly processes.

In addition to this government support, it is also essential to develop public-private partnerships. Companies must understand that their progress cannot be allowed at the expense of ecosystem health. Investments into sustainable practices would be a step for companies toward enhancing their resilience to environmental disruptions while contributing toward the preservation of biodiversity. Embracing circular economy principles—where the crux is waste minimization and subsequent resource reuse—also serves as a beneficial means of making an enormous reduction in the ecological footprint of industries in the bioeconomy.

What excites me about innovation in this landscape is the potential that biotechnology must address some of the most vivid expressions of urgent environmental challenges. For example, advancements in synthetic biology allow for the engineering and development of biobased materials that can replace traditional plastics-named plastic because they ruin everything will provide biodegradable alternatives that reduce pollution and support a better economy through recycling.

To start with, one may also mention the biotechnological potential in the support of sustainable agriculture. The production of genetically modified crops that can resist pests and diseases will help minimize reliance on destructive pesticides and fertilizers, which lead to habitat destruction and loss of biodiversity. These innovations do increase food security but also healthier ecosystems.

Keeping in mind the full potential of the bioeconomy in ASEAN, I remember to talk about the education aspect and awareness. Public consciousness is an influential tool in the pursuit of a more sustainable bioeconomy, providing a better environment for the stewards. Responsibility toward the natural heritage is developed by engaging the communities and letting them know about the value of biodiversity.

More importantly, entrepreneurship and innovation in bioeconomy must be promoted and encouraged to expedite its growth. Support programs for start-ups and small businesses must emphasize a sustainable approach toward a dynamic innovation ecosystem that promotes economic growth without disrupting biodiversity. The

ASEAN region has much talent and creativity and tapping this will be key to building a sustainable bioeconomy.

In conclusion, there is much promise in the future of bioscience in ASEAN but challenges at the same time. Thus, we would grow the bioeconomy and capitalize on the rich biodiversity of the region by trying to face forward the established issues of habitat destruction, invasive species, climate change, and pollution. We see a future where sustainability defines our practices, co-creation breeds innovation, and sustainable practices trigger prosperous economic returns, thus establishing safety and protection for the ecosystems supporting life.

Going forward means more growth aligned with responsible stewardship. I see the landscape of the bioeconomy to be a place where it thrives, feeding the livelihoods of millions while safeguarding the rich biodiversity that marks ASEAN. A resilient and prosperous future will be profitable for people and the planet if we value our natural capital and make sustainability a vital component of our economic strategies. A journey is well worth embarking on by shaping the legacy of our region for generations to come.

As I delve deeper into the intricacies of bioeconomy, I become more enamoured with the diversity of bio-manufactured products now popping up in the markets today. Biofuels and bio-based plastics are only a few examples of the many whose use has the great potential to radically change the course of industries and shape a more sustainable future for our children. For instance, I have learned that in the domain of bio-based substitutes, business is gaining momentum fast.

Companies are increasingly moving to replace petroleum-derived products with those derived from renewable biological sources. For instance, Ford is collaborating with Jose Cuervo, the famed tequila maker. The two companies are exploring whether the agave byproduct left after tequila is made could be used in parts that would go into Ford vehicles. Unlike other conventional petrochemical-based materials, this latest innovation in bioplastic is not only more sustainable but incorporates agricultural byproducts.

The other sector that is contributing to the growth of bioeconomy includes agriculture. Agricultural biotechnology has become a different game in that it has made it possible for the manipulation of crops to harbour specific biological advantages. This encompasses traits like weed resistance and higher temperature tolerance, giving farmers an easy method of withstanding changes in climatic conditions. Utilization of biotechnology by farmers will better help in the reduction of soil tillage, and pesticide applications, and give way to more yields per acre with the same or fewer inputs. This not only means security in food but also ensures sustainable farmlands that keep our natural resources safe.

The innovation of the bioeconomy made by Michelin in collaboration with IFPEN in France is the latest announcement of an industrial scale to produce bio-based butadiene feedstock necessary for rubber manufacturing. Currently, butadiene used in the tyre industry comes from petrochemical sources; this alternative comes with the offering of this more sustainable approach by the new facility. Estimated at 20-30 metric tons a year of chemicals manufactured from bio-based feedstock, this facility demonstrates that biomanufactured materials are feasible for high-demand applications.

Although quite a lot of progress has been recorded so far in the realization of the bioeconomy, several thorny factors must be toned down for full exploitation. One of the main barriers is the regulatory environment surrounding the commercialization of biotechnology. There are insufficient aspects regarding uncertainties and, therefore, barriers against innovators who need to find ways out of the tangled regulatory paths. However, reflecting on this issue makes it crystal clear that there is a need for clear and streamlined regulatory frameworks to support growth in the bioeconomy.

Generally, the average regulatory phase, being some 16.5 years, is quite long enough to be an insurmountable challenge for founders and entrepreneurs looking forward to bringing their innovations into markets. A delay injures creativity and investment by further putting at risk the business's velocity by which it can adjust to changing market requirements. To advance the bioeconomy more quickly, administrations must take concrete policy action regarding the streamlining and expediting of these regulatory pathways.

This is one crucial step in dealing with regulatory challenges: towards a more defined framework for the commercialization of biotechnology. Policymakers need to close ranks with industry players, researchers, and agencies to adopt guidelines that promote innovation in a safe and environmentally friendly manner. With a palatable regulatory environment, we shall enable our founders to transition from ideas to commercially viable manufacturing facilities much more quickly than we are doing now.

Meaningful consultation by the regulators with the stakeholders deepens insight into the concerns and needs of the bioeconomy. It creates trust for the innovators and the regulating bodies while developing constructive policy, especially for either party. Hence, the policymakers through interaction with experts in the business and entrepreneurial sector may gain some insight into specific issues in terms of regulatory hurdles at the bioeconomy level thereby helping to alleviate those growth concerns.

The coming bioeconomy, then, raises important issues related to investment in R&D. Adequate resources for these investments are bound to improve our understanding of biotechnology and its applications, hence leading to more effective regulatory frameworks. Public and private collaboration gives room for innovation and the development of new biotechnologies that could address such challenging conditions as global climatic changes and food insecurity.

Apart from regulations issues, the funding of early-stage biotechnology ventures is a significant challenge. The founders who generate biotechnology ventures cannot attract investors who may be advised against investing in long-term projects with less than certain timeliness. This requires an increase in funding mechanisms to support the unique characteristics that have been identified with biotech startups. All this comes closer to realizing a more robust innovation ecosystem through creating investment models as those assimilated long development timelines associated with the biotechnology venture.

Entrepreneurial culture must be fostered in the bioeconomy. Entrepreneurship education and mentoring that will help early-stage founders learn and navigate the complexities in the biotech landscape will encourage interdisciplinary teamwork between scientists, engineers, and business professionals.

Upon introspection of the key actors of the bioeconomy, it has been manifested that partnership has been a key aspect for overcoming the various challenges surrounding it. Associating firms at any stage in their development---whether well-established or in the start-up phase---synergizes innovation and accelerate commercialization. Established firms have valuable resources, distribution networks, and industry expertise that can be granted to support the startup to scale its operation. It is in this direction that diverse stakeholders will tap into what they are best at and make a collaborative ecosystem work for the forward propulsion of the bioeconomy.

Education is also an important facilitator in the development of a bioeconomy. Education on the potential of biotechnology and bio-manufactured products can help in raising public support and understanding. Education to communities, businesses, and educational institutions helps in building a well-equipped workforce for prospering in the bioeconomy. Public outreach programs can also help to demystify the application of biotechnology by reducing misconceptions and promoting excitement about what is expected from biotechnology.

While opportunities are many, there is much reason for optimism about the potential of the bioeconomy. While acknowledging regulatory challenges and furthering partnership, then fostering entrepreneurship and education, an environment will be generated that is conducive to the encouragement of innovation and sustainable growth. Though the potential of the bioeconomy goes far beyond economic gain, it stands as a pathway to a more sustainable and resilient future for our planet.

In conclusion, the bioeconomy is a robust driver that will be able to change industries, improve food security, and help bring the environment closer to sustainability. However, all individual's policy frameworks, the industry participants, and the public need to chart this transition together as the challenge of its growth is faced. If we work in concert to establish an enabling regulatory regime, drive research and development, and create an entrepreneurship-enhancing culture, the full potential for the bioeconomy will be unlocked. It is a journey requiring commitment and cooperation, but it's a price well taken for the rewards-a more sustainable future for generations to come. Bioeconomy holds the key to a prosperous and resilient world, and it's all our responsibility to see to this end.

Chapter 6: Key Factors for Successful Biotechnology Investments

"An investment in knowledge pays the best interest."

— Benjamin Franklin

In examining the various factors that contribute to the success of biotech investments, I reflect on my extensive experience teaching in numerous management schools globally. Biomedical entrepreneurship is my favourite subject to teach, and in the process, I developed an interest in helping people understand what it takes to make a successful biotech venture and, thereby, how to make the right investments in this space. Investments in biotechnology differ from other technology or services investments due to distinct challenges, risks, and rewards.

From my experience with various global bioeconomies, I developed a framework called **GEM** modules, which stands for "***GOVIN Entrepreneurship Management***." These crucial principles guide me in assessing biotech startups' potential for success.

What are the key factors for successful investment in biotechnology? In this section, I outline some of the most important GEMs from my framework that's serve as fundamental building blocks defining the direction a company will take and the many hurdles inherent in the biotechnology industry.

GEM-1: Vision, Mission, and Values

GEM-2: Founders Integrity and Strength of Management Team

GEM-3: Intellectual Property & Freedom to Operate Analysis

GEM-4: Total Addressable Market (TAM)

GEM-5: Business planning and business models.

GEM-6: Commercialization Strategy

GEM-7: Financial Planning

GEM-8: Exit Strategy

GEM-9: Impact Assessment

GEM-1: Vision, Mission, and Values

One of the first and most important factors to examine before investing in any biotech company is its vision, mission, and values. Understanding the direction a biotech company is taking is crucial when making an investment decision. A company's vision provides a broad picture of what the founders aspire to achieve in the long term. It answers the critical question: Where does the founder see the company going? Without a strong and clear vision, it is hard to feel confident about the long-term prospects of a company.

In biotech, it's even more important because, the journey from idea to market is long, expensive, and replete with uncertainties. However, vision alone is not enough. Equally important, is the mission, since it articulates how this vision is to be achieved. For the mission is the action plan, or at least the blueprint, which describes how one gets from the lab bench to the marketplace. Big ideas are one thing; without a concrete plan for how such big ideas might become real, such big ideas are just so many nightmares.

Also, most biotech companies fail to make good translations from research to commercial products. Besides the vision and mission, values regulating the firm are also key. In investing, the first question I ask myself is: What are the core values of this company? Are they geared towards integrity, merit, trust, or teamwork? In recent years, corporate governance has taken the forefront in my assessment process. I have witnessed many failures of early-stage companies with great products or promising research only because poor corporate governance dominated.

I prioritize evaluating a company's value system before investing.

A company that adheres to ethical principles is well-equipped to navigate the inevitable challenges of the biotech industry.

In the end, a company's vision, mission, and values form the DNA of its culture as well as strategy. They articulate where the organization is headed, the route it will take to get there, and the principles that will guide it on that route. Without these foundational components, no amount of financial investment can ensure success.

GEM-2: Founders Integrity and Strength of Management Team

The second GEM that characterizes my model is about the people behind the company: who founded it, and above all, who manage it. I've learned that a company's success depends on the strength of its team, no matter how great the product or technology is. At Harvard, they explain the necessity of supporting a team of strong management. The logic is simple: markets, technologies, and business environments are always in the process of evolution; a good team can adapt to those changes. A balanced management team can pivot, adjust, and be decisive when its processes must navigate through challenges. For instance, let me give you an example of one of the most famous biotech companies ever—*Genentech*. Genentech was founded way back in the mid-1970s and is widely accepted as the company that started the biotechnology revolution. What is interesting about Genentech is that, although they did have a plan of business at inception, they did not adhere strictly to that plan. A good deal of what was written in their original business plan was not ever consummated. Despite this, the company succeeded. And the reason had to be the strength of its management team.

The founders of Genentech, along with the team they built, were smart. They knew that the biotech industry was fundamentally unpredictable and thus would be willing to adjust the strategy to fit into the market conditions as it evolved. So, this flexibility coupled with their expertise and leaders brought them from a tiny firm to one of the most successful ventures in biotech history.

Genentech was acquired by Roche for an astonishing US $90 billion in 2009. It is one of the biggest deals ever made in biotechnology then, and it depicts the power that good management can add to a company. Even if the product has some inadequacies or the original business plan fails to generate any returns, good management will turn the firm in the right direction by exploiting new avenues and making wise moves.

What qualities should investors seek in a management team? I look for a combination of technical expertise and business acumen. In biotech, it is just not about talent who understand deep-tech science, but equally important are people who know how to navigate the business side—in this case, funding, managing regulatory approvals, or building partnerships with other companies.

Resilience: Becoming a biotech company takes a lot of grit. Companies, after facing challenges such as unsuccessful clinical trials, reduced funding, or regulatory obstacles, often focus on preserving their existing resources. Lastly, I would be remiss in not mentioning leadership and teamwork. The triumphant success of a company will certainly depend on personal talent, but it is also strongly contingent upon the team's functionality as one unit. As I have observed so far, the best successful biotechnology companies in my viewpoint are the ones with an aligned management team on their vision and values and working together to achieve their set goals.

GEM-3: Intellectual Property & Freedom to Operate Analysis

I have always included Intellectual Property (IP) as part of what I emphasize when discussing the key tenet of investing in biotech ventures. It is one of the most important GEM in my framework for identifying successful biotech ventures. If there is no strong IP, then there is no real barrier to entry: the ability of another firm to replicate what a biotech firm is doing and compete with it means that any potential investment's value becomes severely diminished.

Why is intellectual property so important to biotech? Biotechnology companies are almost always built on breakthrough science and disruptive innovation. What you're investing into isn't the product, but the technology: new methods, formulations, and techniques that will change health care or medical treatment. IP means it's an innovation exclusive to the company you're investing in and it provides the competitive edge needed to compete within a very competitive market.

Generally, intellectual property involves three aspects: composition of matter, method of use, and utility. The composition of matter refers to the chemical, biological, or physical entities that a biotech company has come up with. For example, in a new vaccine, this entails the unique formula or the specific components of the vaccine. This invention's composition, method of use, and utility are defined by how it can be applied that is, the specific ways the vaccine is administered or its therapeutic effects. Finally, utility ensures that the invention is useful and solves a specific problem. Without composition, method, and utility, real technological advantage cannot be established.

But just having intellectual property rights isn't enough. What most investors in biotech space want to see is the "*Freedom to Operate*". Essentially, even if a firm holds a patent, they have first to ensure that they are not infringing patents owned by another firm. Without freedom to operate, the firm gets saddled with endless futile legal tangles that prevent them from commercializing their product. However, for any biotech investment to work, intellectual property and freedom to operate should go hand in hand. Hence, biotech founders must work with good patent attorney firms that can provide both a patent analysis as well as freedom to operate analysis report.

One of the challenges I have frequently seen, especially in emerging markets, is that companies are filing for intellectual property only within the country. Domestic patents are important, but they are not enough if the company aspires to become a global player. For major markets like the U.S. and Europe, filing a U.S. Patent Cooperation Treaty application protects intellectual property in multiple countries, expanding reach and attracting larger partners or acquisitions for biotech companies. International patent filings come with their own set of issues, such as cost of filing and managing the patents. The filing and servicing of patents globally consume a lot of resources, which may be cost-prohibitive for an early-stage company. This is another reason why biotech start-ups need grants or funding from universities, research institutions, or government programs that support their patent applications. Otherwise, many promising companies will not be able to grow beyond their home market, which puts a cap on their growth prospects.

GEM-4: Total Addressable Market (TAM)

Successful biotech ventures and ideas are not simply innovative science but about solving a real-world problem. The bigger the problem is, the larger the market size is and the Total Addressable Market (TAM). One of the most common reasons for failure in biotech is that founders become overly enthralled with their solution without ever actually identifying properly what problem they are solving. While many scientists have developed amazing technologies in the lab, they then fail to commercialize them because the market doesn't have a significant need for their solution. Considering this, one should begin with thorough understanding of the problem statement.

Successful biotech companies identify big, pressing problems-often in areas with high unmet medical needs and then develop innovative solutions to address those problems. For instance, for RNA vaccines, the need for effective and speedy vaccine development was highlighted during the COVID-19 pandemic. Companies like *Moderna* and *BioNTech* recognized the problem of fast-spreading viral infections that have limited vaccination solution at hand. They developed cutting-edge RNA technologies and succeeded. The lessons I have learned over the years are that the more enormous the problem, the more likely one is to succeed. In most cases, the risks are higher, and with higher risks come greater rewards. For investors in biotech, one needs to be comfortable with this level of risk as well as understand that the more minute the problem may be, the less impactful it will be on the market.

GEM-5: Business planning and business models.

A good business plan will make a spectacular scientific innovation succeed. Successful biotech companies have business models well-suited to the negotiation of the labyrinthine regulatory environment, procurement of funding, and product launch. For example, a firm producing new therapeutic drugs should have a business plan to account for the extensive clinical trials and regulatory approvals required before that drug could reach the market. For medtech companies, partnerships often are at an early stage and become critical. It is not just about science, but also how the firm is going to validate its technology with its customers, establish partnerships with bigger pharmaceutical or medical device companies, and build a recurring revenue source.

GEM-6: Commercialization Strategy:

How do you get from the bench in the laboratory to the marketplace? The strategy of commercialization varies by the type of biotech company we are working with. Is it a therapeutic, a vaccine, or a medical device company? Each has its way into commercialization.

For therapeutic companies, the most important element of a commercialization strategy is the outcome of the clinical trial data. Without proper safety and efficacy data of a drug, it will never get to the market. Additionally, even a positive data set is considered a substantial regulatory challenge. The regulatory process in the U.S. and Europe is long; however, the benefits warrant going through the trouble since these markets offer the largest and most attractive markets for biotech companies.

Medtech companies, however, tend to be more dependent on partnerships for commercialization. These partnerships can mean partnering with the bigger medical device companies to scale their operations, distribute products, and clear regulatory hurdles.

GEM-7: Financial Planning:

For any biotech investment to work, there needs to be a clear financial plan. What are the revenue projections? What kind of return on investment can investors expect, and when? Biotech has a notorious reputation as a long-term investment requiring several years and significant capital before seeing financial returns. For these reasons, investment in biotech should be managed through realistic financial projections and a well-thought plan for the management of shareholder expectations over time.

In this case, early-stage biotech firms require more than just an exercise in accounting to handle their financials; it's almost the art of delicate strokes. Biotech firms face significant financial challenges because products normally take a great amount of time before they commercialize, meaning there are lengthy periods before much revenue can be garnered. In the biotech industry, it generally takes ten years or more for the product to hit the market. Medtech companies have timelines a little shorter - five to eight years; diagnostics firms tend to have a faster pathway, and most products go to market in five years. This variation in the timeline of commercialization affects the type of financial projections made.

GEM-8: Exit Strategy:

In evaluating a biotech investment, two chief elements that venture capitalists evaluate are Net Present Value (NPV) and Internal Rate of Return (IRR). NPV allows an investor to determine at what value one should invest in a firm. IRR measures the return based on the time the undertaking is expected to take to attain commercialization and eventually exit.

Since IRRs are time-sensitive, the IRR for a biotech company would be dramatically different if it exited in five years versus ten years. However, if the product in question turned out to be a blockbuster, even a ten-year timeline might deliver attractive returns. For instance, examples like BioVex, which became a unicorn, had amazing IRRs despite the protracted timelines. Therefore, financial projections of a biotech company become essential not in terms of revenue but rather in-depth in understanding how complex the problem they are trying to solve would be, the size and type of market, among other things, and for how long it will take to commercialize the product and, therefore, the exit for the investors.

A key component of these financial projections is creating an exit strategy. Investors know when and how to cash out of the investment, and of course, there's high risk in biotech, but it's also highly rewarding. That five-year to ten-year timeline for an exit would be predicated on the company's ability to manage that risk and hit those commercialization milestones. Investing in a biotech firm has a significant risk profile and fewer willing risk-takers, especially outside of established biotech ecosystems, like the United States that has an extremely well-developed biotech ecosystem with deep-tech investors who are willing to take risks on high-potential companies. In Asia, however, biotech ecosystems is still evolving, where investors are not used to high failure rates and long timelines, that explains the difference. It is a function of the environment and market maturity and, therefore, has a direct impact on the kind of exits that companies in different regions may be able to achieve.

GEM-9: Impact Assessment:

Beyond such considerations as financial projections and exit strategies, the impact has increasingly become an important factor in investments in biotechnology. While some investors are focused on generating valuations with a profit-centric model, others also want to make a difference. To achieve this, the impact investment has risen to the fore. Impact investing enables investors to focus their financial objectives with a desire to make a positive difference in society by prioritizing companies and projects that offer social returns complemented by financial returns.

For me, impact investing is one of those areas close to my heart that I've been keenly interested in since I first started investing in biotech and healthcare companies way back in 2001. Making impact investments has one of the most powerful effects possible: the opportunity to make meaningful change. Take for instance a biotech firm that is coming up with cancer treatments. Cancer is a disease that brings about unbearable agony: losing a loved one to cancer is perhaps the worst experience a person may have to endure. The thought of investing in a firm that will, with a probability, develop a cure or effective treatment for this terrible disease is incredibly impactful. No other benefit is greater than knowing that your investments are saving lives and bringing hope to people suffering from this deadliest disease.

Such impact on research and development (R&D) for biotech and healthcare companies is of utmost importance. This means it's never about merely making a profit but changing lives. That is why, despite the financial returns, I remained in this sector, because of its real impact on society. As each discovery brings any new treatment and every successful clinical trial, so does it bringing an essential step closer to solving health issues that plague our community today.

Beyond that impact at an individual level, investments ensure overall ripple effects within society. The result occurs mainly because such investments ensure the general community reaps from advanced health care and biotechnology discoveries. Impact investments contribute to the realization of Sustainable Development Goals (SDG) by driving inclusive and equitable healthcare solutions. Such investments are essential for ensuring long-term sustainability both in terms of economic returns and societal well-being.

Global impact investment initiatives are just one of the important initiatives in this field that offer resources, research, and counselling to investors and organizations interested in creating an impact. It further helps generate awareness and advance the field of impact investing, promising more resources and allocation to such companies that make a difference in healthcare, sustainability, and well-being among communities.

Balancing financial returns with social impact is a very attractive and rewarding challenge for any investor in the biotech business. Focus on impact investment then enables it to contribute to a more sustainable and equitable world. It also opens the possibility of having more investors participate in meaningful kinds of investments that would go beyond making only financial gains. This means that impact investing holds a great opportunity to engage any interested individual or people in the pursuit, and it has become a hot trend for seasoned financial experts and impact philanthropists.

Ultimately, biotech and healthcare investments aim to build a better future. It may be through curing diseases, improving diagnostics, or creating new medical technologies pursued in the interest of creating value beyond the bottom line. The financial projections and the exit strategy are only part of the equation, but it's the ability to come up with products that change lives, contribute to societal well-being, and ensure that a future generation of humanity has better healthcare that leads to success in biotech.

Collaborations are important in impact investments. These collaborations unlock a network of like-minded individuals and institutions who believe in their common aim of creating meaningful and sustainable change. No one can work in isolation in the world of impact investing. The partnership was inevitable in carrying out joint approaches from multiple sources, pooling resources and coming up with solutions that cannot be solved by any single solution. The collaborations help to leverage their resources, expertise, and connections to ensure that their impact investments truly have the possibility of helping to resolve some of the most pressing world problems.

Impact funds are the standout way in which impact investments can be implemented. Impact funds are specific investment vehicles designed to direct financial capital into projects or initiatives that have measurable social and environmental impact. Impact funds pool resources from different investors and achieve economies of scale, thus being able to fund bigger and even more ambitious projects. This allows social impact investors to target areas such as education, health care, renewable energy, and affordable housing among others. These areas are important because they are part of the firmest grounds on which an equitable and sustainable society is built.

Large-scale movers and shakers that are growing the phenomenon of impact investing are social impact investors, who, in essence, align their value with their goal of investment. In other words, they pursue not only financial returns but also opportunities where their money can be a force for good. In it, they fund innovative solutions to some of the most pressing problems in society. By committing their capital and experience, they contribute to a more equitable and sustainable future. In this respect, social impact investors are equally change agents in addition to financiers.

Profit remains a constituent element of an impact investment but leverages over the conventional ideas of profit. Impact investment is the concept of "*profit with a purpose.*" The Rockefeller Foundation, one of the pioneering organizations in the realm, has defined impact investment as providing capital to innovative ventures that advance and leverage their mission for good. Through impact investment with the Rockefeller Foundation, billions of lives have been transformed through improvements in public health, food, clean energy, and financial services. This model shows the idea that good financial success need not come at the cost of social good. Instead, the two work to complement each other, with the potential for sustaining a model for long-term success.

Impact investors and I look for investments using rather rigorous evaluation frameworks. For example, I have developed a nine-gem framework assessing successful investments in life sciences and biotechnology. This holistic approach will hence take into consideration not only financial feasibility but also a project's potential for resultant social and environmental impact. For instance, within the pharmaceuticals industry, we shall have an investment put into companies that specialize in green chemistry* and sustainable pharmaceutical production. Commitment towards sustainability will ensure that the development of products not only serves the health of humanity but also the health of the planet.

Such an integrated approach does, thus provide one fundamental message of impact investment: *bridging profit and purpose.* The model has made remarkable advancements over the years as a sharp tool to address society's medical, educational, and environmental problems. Aligning financial objectives with social or environmental goals creates what is often called a "win-win" situation, where financial returns and social good flow together.

Several key elements distinguish impact investments from traditional investments, and understanding those elements is important to any person looking to invest in this space.

- Profit and Purpose: Impact investing is one way to reconcile profit and purpose and at least two competing realities. It is not "between" profit or social good but "both/and". Not to be giving up the profit for social good but recognizing that profit and social good can coexist. Impact investors, with consideration for market-rate returns and the social benefits of an investment, can develop a value proposition that encompasses both dimensions.

- Social Impact Bonds and Funds: They are financial instruments that support specific social outcomes. For example, a social impact bond may back a project that reduces homelessness or increases educational attainment. These instruments enable investors to give directly to initiatives with measurable and meaningful impacts on society.

- Impact Measurement: A determinant for impact investment is the social and environmental performance of the investment made and its report. Such aspects help in transparency and then accountability so an investor can track the progression of her investments while having a clear understanding of what kind of effects she's being able to make.

So far, my own experience reflects several marquee investments that are translating principles of impact investing. Among the ones I have had the privilege of working with is BioVex, a spin-off from University College London, developing cutting-edge biotechnologies. The other example here is Sun Biomedical (now known as Biosensors International), based in Singapore, which has charted a significant way ahead in medical devices for cardiovascular applications. Just two examples of the kind of innovation that impacts investments that can drive and deliver to society and the planet.

Quintiles is a contract research organization (CRO) located in Research Triangle Park, North Carolina. Quintiles assists pharmaceutical firms in bringing new drugs to market through clinical services. Outsourcing is typically the case in the pharmaceutical industry for clinical trial services, and the work of organizations like Quintiles underscores this approach as driving many life-saving treatments. The acquisition of the company for $1.8 billion is a testament to the effectiveness of impact investing only when it harmonizes with strategic partnerships and innovatory solutions.

Like every other successful investment, Medreich Pharmaceuticals, an India-based firm, was among them. Medrich was a leading pharmaceutical firm that manufactured many widely used anti-infective drugs, primarily Augmentin besides nutritional supplements. This company, operating on a global basis, found success in addressing health needs with a sustainability approach coupled with social impact. Medreich's contribution to Indian healthcare, especially infectious diseases, forms an example wherein impact investments can truly add value to people's lives in the real sense.

Impact investing for sure will have the future of teamwork all the way. Whether it would mean partnership cooperation between investors, businesses, and governments or investment vehicles like impact funds and social impact bonds, the goal will be a more sustainable, equitable world. "Bringing profit and purpose together increases the impact of investors' contributions; if done in earnest, can be transformative, changing the approach to investments as well as their role in society.".

Impact investment collaborations are particularly important because they pool resources, skills, and social networks towards much-needed social and environmental transformation. Impact funds, innovative financial tools, and performance measurement and reporting ensure investors that their investments contribute to a better and more sustainable world. The collaborations established with impact investing will play an increasingly important role in solving the complex challenges humanity faces as a global community.

During my scientific and professional journey, I was fortunate to have several mentors, who played the most pivotal role in shaping my thoughts and approaches toward innovation, leadership, and life itself. There are few people who have left a lasting impression on me because of their works- Dr A.P.J. Abdul Kalam, Mr Ratan Tata, and my father, the (Late) Dr. G.P. Sastry. These people have had an incredible impact not only on my career in biotechnology and life sciences but also on my philosophy.

Dr. A.P.J. Abdul Kalam – The Innovation Leader

Dr. A.P.J. Abdul Kalam, the "Missile Man" of India and former President, was one of the most important persons in my life. I had the good fortune of meeting him in person and discussing with him on many occasions during his lifetime. Each session engraved a deep impact, particularly his emphasis on innovation and intellectual property. I recall one conversation vividly. He said to us, "*The only way you can make a nation strong is through innovation*"."

Those words sank deep into my heart; from that day forward, I dedicated myself to working with intellectual property and pioneering innovation in health care, biotechnology, and even deep technology. The words of Dr Kalam's belief that ideas can do wonders strengthened within me my conviction that science applied toward solving real-world problems, can elevate not just an industry but an entire nation.

I consider innovation, as defined by Dr. Kalam, the tool to bring societal transformation. His thoughts have been driving my mind ever since. He not only encouraged technological advancement but also created a mindset of continuous learning and adaptation. He would comment that innovation isn't confined to one specific discipline and must be there in every aspect of our thinking, starting from scientific research towards facing an everyday challenge. This multi-dimensional approach to innovation sculpted the very ethos of my work in biotechnology and life sciences.

Mr. Ratan Tata - The Humble Visionary

Mr. Ratan Tata is, to me, one of India's most respected industrialists, and yet another person whose life and values have influenced me greatly. What appealed to me is his humility and grace while he is widely accredited for his visionary leadership and the ability to transform Tata Group into a global conglomerate. The first time I was able to interact with him was during his visit to Singapore when he was conferred with honorary citizenship by the Singapore government.

What came through and overwhelmed me was Mr. Tata's attention to detail, but more than that was his kindness and humility. Here was a man who had achieved so much in life, yet he always treated everyone—regardless of their position—with the utmost respect. He was an exemplary leader, not one to use the authority he had but his very humanness and good intentions to inspire people around him. The legendary Tata values that he embodied short, integrity, excellence, and a sense of responsibility toward society-are core principles that I have tried to emulate in my professional journey.

His speech was crystal clear in every conversation, and one could easily recognize his profound understanding of global business, philanthropy, and human relations. He taught me that leadership is not only about the right decision-making but is indeed a bundle of building relationships on trust, sincerity, and a shared vision for the good of society. He could look beyond the immediate gains of business and think about the long-term implications on society-the lesson taught to me and which continues to guide me to this day.

Dr. G.P. Sastry - The Silent Mentor

While Dr Kalam and Mr Tata shaped my professional outlook, my father, Dr G.P. Sastry, has significantly influenced my life in so many ways. He hardly ever spoke much, but when he did, the words I heard cut through me. His guidance was often subtle but greatly impactful. My father was the first one to guide me to a career in biotechnology-a decision that defined my life's work.

If I had to trace it back to 1989, when, due to certain circumstances, I was not able to pursue medicine, , my father nudged me to take up molecular biology and biotechnology as an alternative. His advice came at the very juncture in my life when I needed it the most, and that sent me on the path to where I sit today. Looking back, I realized how wise he was. The nascent stage of that time for biotechnology meant that, while he saw a future for himself in this science, he envisioned its contribution far beyond personal success: contributing to the betterment of society through science.

My father embodied contentment and simplicity. He taught me one of the most valuable lessons life ever bestowed upon me: being content with whatever you have. In a world where everybody chases after more - be it wealth, fame, or power- contentment is seldom seen. My dad had taught me in life that happiness is never discovered in the confines of everything accumulated but in the appreciation of what you already have. This simple yet profound understanding has been one guide with my choices in life and at work to focus on the essentials rather than getting derailed by momentary cravings.

The best lesson I learned from my father was letting go. He always taught that not everything that happens in life goes with you, and when things don't go the way, you want them to, then one needs to let go of all resentment so as not to be left backwards. The skill to detach oneself from the fate that either goes wrong or right has been quite crucial for me-when biotech investment is shrouded in high stakes; sometimes success looks just like failure.

The Collective Influence

All three mentors together—Dr. Kalam, Mr. Tata, and my father—built the person I am today. Dr. Kalam always taught me about innovation and intellectual property; Mr. Tata guided me on how to lead with humility and vision; and my father, the virtues of contentment and letting go. In all directions, these lessons go further than any professional achievement but rather about leading a meaningful, purpose-driven life.

In my work today, be it investing in biotech startups, exploring new scientific innovations, or just seeking to cut through the complexity of life itself, I do so carry the lessons learnt from these magnificent human beings. This continues not just to shape my career but shape my views on how I should contribute to society meaningfully and for that, I remain eternally grateful.

Chapter 7: Learning from Failures

'The greatest glory in living lies not in never falling, but in rising every time we fall.'

– Ralph Waldo Emerson

Failures are often celebrated as stepping stones to success, and this philosophy rings so deep in one of the most transformative events in my life. I found inspiration in the life and teachings of Dr. A.P.J. Abdul Kalam, Former President of India & Missile scientist during a particularly trying period. A pivotal moment etched in the annals of Indian history was in 1979 when Dr. Kalam faced his first major professional failure. He was 47 years old. This was the first time he led a team for ISRO, to send a satellite to space, and this project ended up as a disappointing failure in its attempt because the rocket could not accomplish the mission it had set out for. And so, the failure ended; instead, it became a start, one that redefined Indian space exploration.

What differentiated him was his reaction to this failure. He took this failure in stride. There were no signs of despair because this failure had lessons not just for him but for his whole team. His mentor and boss, Dr. Satish Dhawan, demonstrated leadership during this time. As the media bombarded them with questions, Dr. Dhawan stepped forward, shielded his team and took the entire failure personally: "The same team, which has failed here will succeed in its next adventure.". True to his word, within a year, in 1980, the team had successfully launched a satellite, marking India's entry into the elite club of spacefaring nations. The moment of triumph was celebrated not by Dr. Dhawan taking the limelight but by him passing it to Dr. Kalam, who was asked to address the media and share the victory on behalf of the team.

This narrative taught me a vital lesson: a true leader takes responsibility in times of failure and gives credit to their team in moments of success. Dr. Kalam often cited this episode as a cornerstone of his philosophy, and for me, it became a guiding principle in understanding the dynamics of leadership and perseverance.

As I sit back to reflect on my own life, the echoes of failure have been familiar companions in shaping my character and instilling resilience. My failures weren't of national significance like Dr. Kalam, but they were deeply personal, leaving indelible marks on my journey. When I was in school, I was far from being an extraordinary student. I was neither gifted with intelligence nor blessed with high grades. I was instead an average student who studied diligently but without distinction. My whole years at primary school and secondary high school were at par, and even the 10th standard examinations did not help to uplift my otherwise lacklustre performance.

I was thus expecting things to change around my Junior College years (11th and 12th standards). All my energies and hopes were then dedicated to securing a place in medical school. The pressure was tremendous, not just from the competitive environment but also from the expectations of my family. My heart sank when the results of the medical entrance examination came in, and I did not make it to an MBBS program due to non-local quota issue in my home state of Andhra Pradesh, India. It was absolutely crushing.

My mother, one of the strongest people most of the time, could feel the tremors beneath her calm demeanour. Her tears and sharp words pierced me in a way I hadn't anticipated. My father was quiet but said little. The disappointment was unspoken, however. I thought I'd failed not only myself but my entire family. All these expectations in my head added to my self-doubt, plummeting me into this dark abyss of despair. In the unbearable sight of tears in my mother's eyes or the heaviness of my father's silence, I walked out of home towards the streets of Hyderabad without knowing my destination.

In this midst of chaos, I found my footsteps take me to the famous "Shivam Temple "at Hyderabad. Its architecture had such a strong resemblance to Lord Shiva's sacred Shiva Linga that I felt a sudden urge to enter. A hesitant step into the unknown became a transformative experience. Inside, the air was soothing with the sound of bhajans, which seemed to rise and fall like waves of comfort washing over me. The scent of incense blended with the rhythmic clinking of bells, producing an atmosphere that was calming and profound. For the first time in days, I felt a semblance of peace.

Tears streamed down my face as I let go of all that pent-up emotion. It was in this temple that I heard the teachings of Sri Sathya Sai Baba, India's most revered spiritual teacher. Shirdi Sai Baba and Puttaparthi Sri Sathya Sai Baba became both sources of comfort and direction for me. I regularly attended the bhajans on Thursdays at the temple, drawing strength from the prayers as well as the community surrounding me. The session would culminate with a discourse or a simple thought for the day; these words proved to be quite strength for me as I continued attending the bhajans regularly.

The temple became a sanctuary, to which I could go and sit in judgment of my failure without fear of judgment to slowly rebuild my sense of self-worth. By this time, I had enrolled in an undergraduate program in Microbiology Botany & Chemistry at Nizam College, Osmania University in Hyderabad. It was not what I had had in mind for myself, but at least it was forward. For all three years of my Graduate college, the temple remained my anchor. Prayers, bhajans, and teachings by Sai Baba infused in my mind a sense of resilience and purpose. Looking back, those years were a crucible that forged a stronger, more determined version of myself. The failure to secure a spot in medical school, which once felt like the end of the world, became a turning point. It taught me the value of perseverance, the importance of seeking solace in spirituality, and the strength that comes from embracing rather than avoiding failure.

Dr. Kalam's story of a transition from failure to success is what I have learned during my journey to overcoming difficulties in life. Failure becomes merely a detour. Reassessing, recalibrating, and rising stronger have been my approaches to my own personal failures toward creating a brighter future. Just as I read about Dr. Kalam transforming a national setback into his most historic achievement, Dr. Kalam and I became able to transform their failures into steppingstones to an even brighter future for our country.

At the crossroads of life, I had no other option than to pursue Graduate degree programme in Microbiology at Nizam College at Hyderabad, India. Medicine has been alluring to me for years because of the vision it created about it. But life, had manoeuvred me onto this different lane. My parents, seeing my emotional turmoil, decided to take the charge. My father, with a silent resolve in his eyes, made this choice for me. My mother, being as practical as ever, applied on my behalf. I was by no means willing to engage in the idea, but at that time, they insisted on letting go of something and moving on with a new emerging subject, Microbiology.

Nizam College had recently started its graduate program; a new combination of Microbiology, Botany and Chemistry offering a degree in Bachelor of Science. It wasn't my dream, but it was an opportunity. I reluctantly started the three-year course with a heavy heart yet determined to make some use of it. And when I started studying for it, a spark of interest started to flicker within me. The world of DNA, microorganisms, the chemistry of life, and the wonders of botany were, without a doubt, interesting. But I could never see this as anything but a consolation prize, a reminder that I had failed at something.

Those three years weren't just about academics; they were about transformation. I poured myself into the work, finding solace in the rigours of the program. The daily prayers at the Shivam temple continued to anchor me, offering me the strength to navigate my internal struggles. Slowly, the bitterness of failure gave way to resilience. I began to realize that this new path, though unintended, was shaping me in ways I hadn't anticipated.

Post successful completion of my graduate degree program, I appeared for the national entrance examination for entry into a Masters' program in Biotechnology. Conducted by Jawaharlal Nehru University (JNU) in New Delhi, it was a fiercely competitive exam with only 100 scholarships available across the country. The added pressure came in the form of those who topped the ranks being offered scholarships. The stakes were high; I was not going to be a participant in history repeating itself.

The memory of my earlier failure acted as a great motivator. I buried myself in preparation, studying with a tenacity that I hadn't known I had within me. The long hours spent studying were gruelling, but I was fueled by deep-seated resolve. Every moment spent with books meant that I was further away from the despair of the past and closer to redeeming myself in my eyes.

This moment, when the results came out, cannot be explained in words; it felt more like a feeling of relief and victory. I got the 23rd rank nationwide, something which felt almost like a miracle. For the first time in years, I was filled with pride. The scholarship attached with my admission to the Masters' programme in Molecualr Biology & Biotechnology at the prestigious GB Pant University in Pantnagar, India, was not just about financial aid; it proved to be a validation of the hard work and perseverance through which I had reached such a level. Prof Govind Krishan Garg, Head of Department of Biotechnology at the University called me to inform me that my application was ranked 1st in the University. It was a turning point—a moment wherein failure turned out to be a steppingstone to success.

As I reflected on my journey, I realized that failure has been my most profound teacher. It humbled me, tried me, and ultimately made me stronger. But the stories of other trailblazers who had faced such setbacks and overcome them only began resonating with me on an even more profound level. Steve Jobs was shown the door of his company; later, he led Apple to unprecedented heights. The world had questioned Walt Disney's creativity, and it had built an empire of imagination inspiring generations still.

But how much closer was the story of Dr. A.P.J. Abdul Kalam, that beacon of hope and resilience?

His first project as the director of ISRO had failed in 1979, which was a bitter pill for the whole nation to swallow. But within a year, he again took the same team to successfully launch a satellite that brought India into the global space race.

The realization dawned on me that failure isn't a mark of inadequacy; it's a rite of passage for anyone striving for greatness. The stories of Walt Disney, Henry Ford, and J.K. Rowling were stories of success but chronicles of perseverance. Every rejection and every misstep were a chapter in their journey that made the eventual triumph even more meaningful. The Wright brothers, who were dismissed as dreamers, proved sceptics wrong by taking humanity to the skies. Michael Jordan cut from his high school basketball team, became a legend by channelling his failure into an unrelenting drive for excellence.

I resonated more with those stories like when legendary India actor Amitabh Bachchan's baritone voice was rejected by All India Radio but is now the signature for that voice, and how it inspired me the way some of those stories said, which wasn't an inspiration only but a reflection of that universal truth. Failure, it says here, isn't the opposite of success but a path to achieve success.

The more I progressed, the more these lessons became a part of me. With every challenge, every doubt that crept in became an opportunity to remind me of what I had learned from my journey and other people's journeys. I no longer fear failure. Rather, it was a companion, a guide, and, ultimately, a teacher who pushed me to grow in ways success never could.

Now that I look back, I think that joining the Nizam College microbiology program, though hesitant in the beginning, really shaped my journey to discovering self-resilience. Not that the path was what I thought it would be; instead, it was what I needed to have it happen. It taught me that failure is not an endpoint but rather a detour on which we can recalculate and steer us toward unimaginable possibilities.

It was through embracing my failures that I found my strength. And that was when I realized the infinite potential each one of us has in rising above setbacks and redefining success on our own terms.

Failures should never deter a person, particularly an entrepreneur, from pushing forward. It is acceptable, even expected, to stumble, but it is never acceptable to quit. In the world of startups, where dreams clash with harsh realities, the most common cause of failure is often attributed to a singular and unforgiving factor: *lack of funding.*

Funding is the lifeblood of any startup, especially in its nascent stages. From inception to exit, a company must traverse a treacherous path often referred to as the "valley of death." This critical phase begins when a prototype is built but requires substantial investment to transform it into a viable product. Many startups falter here, unable to muster the necessary resources to cross the chasm. However, in the realm of biotechnology and life sciences investments, the reasons for failure transcend mere financial scarcity.

Biotechnology startups face unique challenges that demand more than just funding. A visionary founder with the capability to translate ideas from the lab bench to the marketplace is often the keystone of success. Over the last two decades, I invested in a series of biotech ventures, and I began to attribute successes and failures to the ability of the founder. The inability of the founder to raise capital, articulate vision to stakeholders, or create a clear product development plan with market attractiveness can doom otherwise promising ventures.

Through these years, I've witnessed cases that remain etched in my memory, not as failures but as valuable lessons. Take, for instance, *Corgentech Inc*, a Stanford University spinoff with a compelling scientific proposition. The company focused on developing therapeutics for coronary artery bypass graft failure and peripheral artery bypass graft failure, a significant medical need with lucrative market potential. It was headed by Prof. Victor Dzau, a highly respected scientist from Stanford, whose reputation lent credence to the venture.

Corgentech started on a trajectory of great promise. Science was solid, the marketplace was huge, and the company quickly signed its first contract with Bristol-Myers Squibb (BMS) valued at more than $200 million. Suddenly, Corgentech hit the headlines. The company quickly went public, and the IPO was extremely successful. As a result, the price of stock shot upward, reflecting what the market would say about the future of the company.

However, as with many biotech ventures, the tides shifted abruptly. A few months post-IPO, BMS announced that the lead candidate from Corgentech's pipeline failed to demonstrate superior efficacy. This bombshell revelation shattered investor confidence, causing the stock to plummet significantly. For me, this episode served as a harsh lesson in investment strategy. I vividly recall watching the company share price grow from $20 per share to $25 per share. I had planned the investment exit around its fair price of $28 per share. That moment never came. Instead, I learned a fundamental rule of investing: book your profits when you have them. Greed can often be the enemy of success.

Biotech investments are precarious not just due to financial risks but also because of the inherent challenges of product development and timing. Another case that underscores this reality is *Agilix Inc,* a spinoff from the University of Connecticut, New Haven, USA. The company specialized in DNA arrays and protein arrays, technologies that held immense promise during the early stages of genomic research. Agilix had ample cash reserves. Its founder, however, was a perfectionist, hesitant to allocate sufficient resources to accelerate product development.

This cautious approach proved detrimental. Science and technology evolve at a relentless pace, and Agilix found itself outpaced. When the human genome was fully sequenced, the market's interest in DNA arrays diminished rapidly. Although Agilix had ventured into protein arrays, the market was not yet ready to embrace this innovation. The window of opportunity closed, leaving Agilix to sell its assets to PerkinElmer.

This experience taught me another critical aspect of biotech investments: the importance of timing- *A great idea, even with robust funding, can falter if it lacks the market's readiness!* Agilix was not a complete failure, but it fell short of the groundbreaking success it could have achieved. The founder was unable to move decisively, coupled with the rapidly changing landscape, turned potential triumph into mediocrity.

These examples, sobering as they are, reveal an important truth: failures are the building blocks of success. They underscore the intricacies of entrepreneurship, especially in biotechnology, where the stakes are high and the path to market is fraught with uncertainties. Startups in this space require not only significant funding but also visionary leadership, agile decision-making, and an acute awareness of market dynamics.

Building a biotech company is like navigating through a minefield, requiring accurate steps, foresight, and resilience at every corner. Lessons from failures teach founders, investors, and other stakeholders invaluable guideposts - that while success is a great destination, failure oftentimes teaches the most profound lesson.

The journey of startups, especially in the biotech and health-tech sectors, is as treacherous as it is exciting. It often serves as a testament to the delicate balance between vision, execution, and survival in a competitive landscape. Take, for instance, the case of a company that, despite having substantial cash reserves, failed to establish itself as a successful entity. The lesson here is profound, beyond just beating or trailing the market, it is about riding with the market at its proper time. Timing and responsiveness are both essential, but prudent financial management, especially where a firm has the wherewithal but lacks the strategic thought to use such resources is vital.

One such example is a medical imaging and health informatics startup in India. The investment was made in 2016. At face value, everything looked positive. The company had entered partnerships with some of the giant partners and some established hospitals in medical imaging. The partnerships, therefore, were quite enticing, and we felt the company was well on a growth trajectory.

But as time elapsed, cracks in the facade began to show. The founder frequently asked for more funds, which is a red flag we can't ignore. On closer examination, we found that it wasn't a lack of potential or even a lack of effort, but a very glaring lack of financial management acumen. The company had alarmingly large accounts receivable. To put it simply, accounts receivable is money due from customers to a company for services that have been provided or for products that have been supplied. In this case, these amounts were past due.

When we did an *ageing analysis*-the analysis of how long receivables are outstanding, it became clear. For the ideal situation, 1 month is acceptable but for this business, the ageing analysis gave an ugly picture. The delayed payments had been piling up for six months to even one year. The cash flows went down the drain, and the company ended up penniless although their books showed revenues. At last, this management practice saw the end of the company, as such a lesson on financial control and operational supervision is rather harsh.

The dynamics between the founders, particularly in startups with more than one co-founder, is another highly significant challenge.

Industry proverb: "More than two founders and it becomes a zoo." There's nothing really to argue for this other than that it's plain logic; too many people have too much control over decision-making, which brings in bad intentions and egos that do not contribute to the stabilization of the venture.

This was seen firsthand in a pharmaceutical company, where one of the cofounders turned hostile towards the CEO, who was the main founder. The case resulted in a bitter power struggle driven by greed and personal ambition. A hostile co-founder wanted to oust the CEO, creating chaos in the company's growth and a climate of mistrust. As a board member, I stepped in to analyse the situation. I could see that the CEO was honest and committed to the company's mission. Thus, under pressure, the board decided not to entertain the displacement strategy, ensuring integrity and stability. This incident instilled an invaluable lesson in me about investing in firms with too many co-founders; it's relatively easy to get led astray from the underlying objectives of the venture. In addition to these operational concerns, critical oversight often found in startups, especially within biotech, is the fact that there is not a sufficiently strong financial team.

Many founders excel in their technical or product-focused roles but fail to see the importance of a competent Chief Financial Officer (CFO) or finance manager. Most companies let their startups rely solely on chartered accountants and mistakenly think it is a means of having a strategic finance leader on board. However, a CFO plays a completely different role, working closely with the CEO and other executives to develop and execute financial strategies that align with the company's long-term goals. The strategic insights a CFO brings are indispensable.

They don't just manage numbers; they analyse market conditions, forecast financial trends, and identify funding opportunities. This level of experience is particularly critical in biotech, where the road from an idea to market often requires much time and capital. Startups lack a robust financial leader who can represent financial data in a manner that makes investors comfortable, thereby missing key opportunities to raise capital. This gap frequently turns fatal for promising ventures. Equally overlooked is the value of mentorship and a great board of directors. Investors have a lot at stake concerning the quality of a company's board as it speaks to a startup's credibility and strategy. A robust board is populated by professionals who l lend their industry expertise but, more importantly, their name to the venture. That willingness to affix one's name often serves as an implicit recommendation of a venture's merits.

In my experience, startups that attract high-calibre board members tend to instil greater confidence in investors. A well-constituted Board of Directors not only provides valuable guidance but also acts as a safeguard, ensuring that the company adheres to ethical and professional standards. For this reason, I've always made it a point to evaluate the Board's composition as a critical metric before investing in any startup.

These lessons learned from experience depict several kinds of challenges that startups undergo. Winning in this space involves much more than a great idea or significant funding. It often requires a balance of prudent finance, good leadership, and strategic alignment with market needs. Fostering an integrity and trust environment within the company and outside it also cuts across.

While the stories of these companies are full of failure, each failure has been a valuable teacher in shaping how I approach investments and the way I evaluate startups. The journey of navigating these challenges has sharpened my understanding of the intricacies of the biotech and health-tech sectors, but perhaps even more so, has reinforced the timeless truth that success in any venture is as much about resilience and adaptability as it is about vision and innovation.

One of the most important things to ensure the financial health of a startup is to understand, design, and structure a *capitalization table* when raising funds over multiple rounds. The capitalization table, also known as the cap table or shareholders' table, outlines how much money has been invested, at what price, and the resulting valuation of the company. This table serves as a financial blueprint, guiding the startup through its fundraising journey. Yet, many founders misunderstand or mishandle its importance, leading to critical missteps that could jeopardize their ventures.

One recurring issue I've observed is the tendency among founders to artificially overstate their company's valuation, operating under the misconception that a higher valuation automatically translates to better opportunities. They believe that the high valuation of their startup will make it more attractive to investors. Although this would result in short-term benefits in terms of flashy headlines or greater attention, long-term effects can be destructive. In the early stage, when a company sets a very high valuation, subsequent rounds can put the company in a very precarious position. If the company cannot sustain its growth to justify the valuation, then it is forced into a down round—a scenario where the startup raises funds at a valuation lower than the previous round. A down-round can be damaging, not just financially but also reputationally, signalling instability or poor performance to potential investors.

Avoiding these pitfalls requires careful structuring of a cap table that is realistic and thought through. The founders should strike a balance between getting enough capital to support the vision while keeping the valuation fair and reflecting on the status and prospects of the company. A comprehensive understanding of financial strategy, market dynamics, and investor expectations is essential, which many scientific founders without business experience unfortunately lack.

Startups fail not due to a lack of good business ideas or plans but on the part of the founders to effectively execute their vision. Execution is the link that bridges the innovative idea with concrete results. Oftentimes, the vision is exciting; however, if it cannot be well put into words or articulated with a roadmap to execute it, it is only a vision. Execution and a healthy value system are on a similar footing. Investors today are looking into the moral and ethical structure under which a company operates. Founders without a clear value system never manage to gain the trust needed to raise huge amounts of capital. Corporate governance no longer becomes an option that investors can choose to omit; rather, it becomes a value added to the importance of integrity and transparency.

It is not just holding values but also the effective communication and dissemination of the mission, vision, and principles of a company to stakeholders. Often, the heart of a successful partnership revolves around an alignment between the founders' ethos and investor expectations.

Risk management is the other factor to consider for any startup's success. Founders must become adept at not only forecasting potential pitfalls but also finding ways to pass through them. Risk rears its head at many different levels: from an incompetent management team to values misalignment between investors and founders. For instance, it's not uncommon for founders, in their haste to secure funding, to accept investments from parties who lack an understanding of the startup's specific industry needs. This is particularly true for biotech startups, which often require "patient capital." The long gestation periods for product development and regulatory approvals necessitate investors who are willing to wait for returns, often over six to eight years or more. Partnering with the wrong investor can lead to unnecessary pressure and misaligned priorities, further increasing the risk profile of the startup.

Another part of risk management is how the finances are handled. Founders need to learn how to manage finances prudently and cash burn. Overspending, especially immediately after raising capital, drains resources prematurely, leaving the company vulnerable to cashflow crisis. At the opposite extreme is a startup that is too miserly, especially in product development areas. By the time its product finally hits the market, it may be well out of date. After all, timing is everything from timing the product development cycle to knowing how much money to use on when.

Risk management is not simply related to operational decisions but also has something to do with externalities such as political stability and even exit strategies. Political instability in a target market can deter investors and disrupt operations, making it a crucial consideration for expansion plans. Similarly, every investor thinks about the endgame- how and when they will exit the investment. Planning for an exit from the very beginning is as important as setting up the business itself. Without a clear, well-researched exit strategy, a startup risks losing investor confidence, no matter how promising the initial promise.

Any other major red flag is one in which the same founder tries to be both the CEO and chairman as well as even CFO at the same time. Such an individual tends to have a controlling personality type that is likely to repress growth, innovation, and governance.

The concentration of power always defeats the intent of checks and balances for ensuring smooth operations in any organization. As an investor, I've always preferred companies where these roles are independently defined and executed. A chairman with industry expertise can provide invaluable guidance to the CEO while ensuring the board operates effectively. Similarly, a dedicated CFO ensures robust financial management, allowing the CEO to focus on vision and strategy.

The wisdom of great business leaders influences how I evaluate startups. For instance, Jack Welch profoundly impacted my mentor Goran Malm. He taught me two core philosophies. The first, called "*Ipoh Ipoh*," involves starting small with gradual steps to stay on track. As he says, "It's a marathon, not a sprint."

The second principle is "*Keep It Simple and Stupid*". Simplicity in business planning leads to clarity and focus. Straightforward plans are often the most effective, as they can be easily understood by both investors and team members, making them adaptable and scalable for success.

Here is a summary of the some of my investee companies that have failed:

1. Agilix Inc, USA: Medtech company failed due to long-product development timelines
2. Corgentech Inc, USA: Biotech company failed due to the lack of proper efficacy data in Phase 2 and thereby withdrawl of pharm company as a partner
3. Replidyne Inc, USA: Biotech company focused on anti-infective therapeutics failed due to lack of regulatory approval from the USFDA

4. Merlion Pharma, Singapore: Natural products drug discovery company failed due to lack of traction in its pipleine and lack of growth capital
5. Yolopay, Singapore: Founders inability to raise growth capital
6. Mindwave, Singapore: Founder, management conflict and financial mismanagement
7. Renovo, Manchester: Failure of clinical trials in Phase 2
8. Tau Therapeutics, Aberdeen: Long development timelines and lack of regulatory approval
9. CellBeans, India: Business and financial management issues
10. Greenline Labs, India: Founders inability to overcome the valley of death in their product development journey.

Ultimately, a startup's journey from an idea to success depends entirely on balancing vision with execution and ambition with realism and the governance of innovation. So those who understand these lessons and diligently apply them form businesses, but more importantly, a legacy. Focusing on the fundamentals—structuring a thoughtful cap table, ability to raise capital, fostering strong value systems, managing risks effectively, and keeping the business models simple—startups can navigate the complexities of entrepreneurship and pave the way for sustainable growth and impactful exits.

Chapter 8: Defying Prejudices against Biotech Investments

"In investing, what is comfortable is rarely profitable."

— Robert Arnott

Investing in biotechnology ventures is not only tough but risky too as the failure rates during drug development are high. It is a game of high risks and high rewards, where even the best investors can go wrong. Several people have entered the fray, with the hopes of discovering earth-shattering inventions and getting rich but have left with empty pockets after being disillusioned by the complexities of science and business.

Yet, in my journey, I've been fortunate to not only see good returns but also witness unicorn exits, moments that define a career in this volatile industry.

What went right?

As I look back, several key factors have consistently contributed to successful investments in the biotech realm. These factors form the foundation of what it takes to navigate high-risk projects and transform them into high-return ventures.

TEAM: The most critical of these, for me, is the track record of the founder and quality of the management team. The ability of a team to execute the vision, manage intricate risks, or strategize through challenges often determines the fate of a biotech endeavour.

This realization has been shaped by countless experiences. Take the example of *Idun Pharmaceuticals*, for instance. *Idun* was born out of the work of Prof Robert Horvitz from MIT, USA along with Prof John Reed, Burnham Cancer Research Centre, San Diego, USA. I recall my early conversations with Prof Horvitz at his Biology lab at MIT, where we evaluated several of his patents on caspase inhibitors for the treatment of alcoholic hepatitis and liver cirrhosis. It was mutually agreed to raise USD 20 Million at a pre-money valuation of USD 22 million. Early in our journey, we did not recruit a Chief Medical Officer (CMO) with the hope that the Chief Scientific Officer (CSO) would oversee both the science experiments as well as the clinical trials. At first glance, it seemed like a practical choice—an efficient way to centralize responsibility. However, as the company evolved, it became clear that the need for design, planning and monitoring of clinical trials was distinct and required dedicated attention. We pivoted, bringing on a Chief Medical Officer (CMO) to specifically handle the clinical trials, giving the CSO to focus on technological innovations. That decision not only streamlined our operations but also enhanced the quality of our outputs, allowing both domains to thrive under specialized leadership. Post completion of Phase I and Phase 2a trials, Idun Pharma was acquired by Pfizer, and all early-stage investors exited with significant returns.

Subsequently, Prof Robert Horvitz was awarded Nobel prize in medicine for his pioneering work on cell apoptosis.

Similarly, in the case of *Replidyne*, an anti-infective company based in Denver, Colorado, the importance of a well-rounded management team became even more apparent. One of the lead investors, Texas Pacific Group (TPG), understood the value of domain expertise. They appointed Dr Geoff Duyk, a biologist with deep knowledge of anti-infectives to the company's board, ensuring the management team had guidance grounded in scientific understanding. As we neared the exit phase, we recognized the need for strong regulatory expertise and brought on regulatory managers to steer the company through the labyrinth of approvals. Unfortunately, despite our best efforts the lead compound of Replidyne did not meet USFDA approvals, despite successfully completing Phase 3 trials. The strategic decisions, made at critical junctures, highlighted the power of assembling the right people at the right time.

This experience taught me that the composition of a management team should evolve with the company's lifecycle. Early-stage biotech firms may require visionary scientists and entrepreneurs, while growth and exit stages demand seasoned professionals with regulatory, operational, and market expertise. Beyond the management team, the role of a robust board of directors cannot be overstated.

In successful biotech and pharmaceutical investee companies, the Board of Directors wasn't just a formal requirement—it was a powerhouse of industry veterans who brought a wealth of knowledge and networks. We also implemented a Scientific and Industry Advisory Board when needed, leveraging their expertise to navigate complex challenges.

The diversity of these structures, whether supervisory boards, advisory boards, or directorial boards, was tailored to the company's needs. This adaptability ensured that no matter the stage or market, the company was equipped with the intellectual capital required to succeed. Ultimately, having a management team with relevant functional expertise, backed by a strong board, became the cornerstone of successful investments.

SCIENCE: The second pillar of success lies in the novelty of science. In biotech, science is the heart and soul of enterprise. No amount of financial manoeuvring or strategic planning can compensate for weak science. The innovation itself must be disruptive, compelling, underpinned by rigorous research and a clear path to application. It doesn't just mean a breakthrough drug or therapy; it means evidence that science is robust enough to withstand not only the scrutiny of regulators and investors but, ultimately, also the market.

I have seen firsthand how scientific excellence makes or breaks an investment. The quality of the research team, the methodology they apply, and the clarity of objectives determine the potential of the company. Investors often get carried away with the excitement of a new idea without fully understanding its feasibility. It is here that diligence and experience come into play. Knowing when to ask hard questions, when to demand more data, and when to walk away are all skills honed over years in the field. When these two elements-the strength of the management team and the quality of the science-align lay the foundation for success.

But even then, there is no guarantee. The biotech industry is fraught with uncertainty, from regulatory hurdles to market dynamics, and navigating these challenges requires not just skill but resilience. Over the years, I've learned that the ability to adapt, pivot, and persevere is often what separates a promising biotech company from a successful one. As much as the biotech industry may require scientific savvy, managing people and processes often represents more than half of my investment journey. It's understood that there's rarely ever just one genius stroke in getting success here. Instead, it is the ultimate result of thorough planning, non-stop execution, and a commitment to the vision.

As I reflect on the factors that have led me to the successes, I'm reminded that these lessons, though hard-earned, are what make the pursuit of biotech investments so uniquely rewarding.

GLOBAL PATENTS & FREEDOM TO OPERATE: Quality of science is the bedrock of any successful biotech investment. The world of intellectual property drives a given industry, and strong patents for a company often make all the difference between their success or failure. A great patent portfolio offers both legal protection and a strategic advantage: ensuring that the exclusive innovations of the company are defensible. These patents must not only be granted but also demonstrate a robust "freedom to operate."

This means that the company's inventions are free from overlapping claims by other patents, avoiding potential legal entanglements. Evaluating this aspect is paramount because, without it, the investment is exposed to risks that can undermine even the most groundbreaking discoveries.

Biotech investments are highly competitive by nature. The landscape is a battlefield where only those armed with strong patents and a solid intellectual property strategy can hope to emerge victorious. In this competitive game, success often hinges on exclusive ownership of innovation and freedom to operate in various markets of interest.

However, the lines blur when it comes to service-based companies such as those offering pharma, biotech, or clinical services. Here, intellectual property isn't the sole determinant of success. Factors like operational speed and the management team's capability to systematically execute projects become equally critical. For such companies, the race is not only about owning proprietary technology but also about outpacing competitors in efficiency and delivery.

Beyond intellectual property, another vital factor in biotech investment is the ability to interpret and analyse clinical data effectively. This becomes especially crucial in projects transitioning from preclinical research to clinical trials. The journey from filing an Investigational New Drug (IND) dossier to completing safety trials (phase one), efficacy trials (phase two), and ultimately pivotal trials (phase three and phase four) requires meticulous planning and execution. Each phase generates mountains of data, and within this data lies the key to understanding the viability of the molecule or therapeutic approach.

A critical component of this analysis is understanding statistical measures like the P-value and P-coefficient. These metrics help quantify the deviations in trial data, revealing whether the outcomes are statistically significant or merely the result of random chance. The ability to interpret these numbers is not just a skill but an art, requiring a deep understanding of clinical trial design and execution.

Questions such as how the trials were planned, which Contract Research Organization (CRO) executed them, and what kind of data emerged can significantly influence the perceived success of the clinical experiments.

The other skill in analysing the data of trials is the scrutiny of the reliability of the CROs involved. These organizations are very important to ensure that trials are conducted scientifically and ethically.

Their reputation and track record often determine the quality and reliability of the data generated. This translates to an investor digging into all the details of the trial process, from the selection of participants to the methodologies used, so that clinical outcomes are robust and credible. The ability to raise capital is also equally critical as it can make or break even the most promising biotech ventures.

FUNDING: Many biotech companies don't fail because their science isn't good enough; they fail because they run out of money. This industry is the epitome of deep-tech investments, requiring substantial funding to sustain long-term development.

To take a molecule from the animal testing or pre-clinical stage through human clinical studies- phase one (for safety), phase two (for efficacy), and phase three (pivotal efficacy) trials, a company might need upwards of $40 to $50 million, depending on the size of the trial and the country where the trial is being conducted. At times, even higher investments are necessary. In fact, clinical trials are a much more feasible undertaking at one-fifth of the costs associated with those conducted in emerging markets such as India, but more work needs to be done to build trust in data collection and regulatory compliances for a global trial also with data being collected from the from U.S. or European centres.

So, while savings in terms of costs can be there, there needs to be proper balance and harmony among companies while considering these aspects. Partnering with the right CROs that operate in emerging and developed markets is necessary. Such companies can provide data of prime quality necessary for regulators but will also work on cost optimization. But raising capital is not only about raising millions of dollars; it is about raising money at the right time from the right expert investors. Investors in the biotech space need to be savvy enough to understand the nuances of funding rounds, valuations, and strategic partnerships. This type of smart capital isn't just fuel for the journey; it's a sign of credibility that attracts further investment and support. Without it, even the most innovative companies can find themselves struggling to survive.

BUSINESS MODELS: Traditionally biotech and pharma companies have followed a FIPCO model – Fully-integrated Pharma company which incurs lots of capex and manpower costs but low focus on product development or innovation. Now, the emphasis is more on VIPCO model- Virtually Integrated Pharmaceutical company, where the focus is innovation through collaborations and building a virtually integrated value chain. In future, there will be more emphasis on the NRDO model- No Research, Development only model; in such a scenario the R&D will be taken by academia and philanthropy-driven public-sector research. Major pharma companies are already pivoting to managing late-stage product portfolios for optimal financial returns.

The financial models for drug development will evolve too with new business models. For example, Option-based financing and royalty-based financing are two clear business models that will be preferred by investors.

EXIT STRATEGIES: Finally, the goal of any investment is to secure a successful exit. In the biotech world, this could be an acquisition, a merger, or an Initial Public Offering (IPO). The ability to navigate the exit process is as critical as the initial investment decision. A successful exit not only validates the investment but also ensures significant returns for stakeholders.

It's the moment when years of meticulous planning, funding, and execution culminate in tangible success. An exit, however, is only possible with the best preparation and foresight. This means placing the company in such a position that it will attract buyers or investors. For example, one can achieve major milestones, gain regulatory approvals, or even show commercial viability.

In the end, biotech investment is a complex and multifaceted endeavour. It's a journey that requires a deep understanding of science, business, and strategy. From evaluating intellectual property to interpreting clinical data, from raising capital to securing exits, every step is a test of skill, judgment, and perseverance. The rewards are immense, but so are the challenges. Yet, for those willing to embrace the risks, the potential for impact—both financial and societal—is unparalleled.

As an investor, one of the most valuable lessons in the intricate world of biotech investments is the importance of maintaining emotional neutrality. It may sound simple, but in practice, it is far from easy. Biotech ventures often carry an aura of promise, of hope—sometimes even the potential to revolutionize healthcare as we know it. Yet, as an investor, it's imperative to resist the allure of these narratives. Never fall in love with a biotech company or an investment decision too much. Emotional attachment clouds judgment, and in this high-stakes game, clarity is paramount.

When I say this, I mean that every decision must be rooted in rational analysis and strategic foresight. It starts with evaluating the entry point of your investment, understanding the valuation, the milestones, and the risk factors at the time of purchase. Equally, it means defining the exit point with a clear-eyed perspective. Biotech investments are not about riding the wave forever or waiting for that golden moment when the molecule in development secures market approval. Often, that moment may never come. Regulatory hurdles, unforeseen clinical trial outcomes, or shifts in market dynamics can derail even the most promising molecules.

The safer, and often more rewarding, strategy lies in knowing when to step away. If you're sitting on profit, my advice has always been simple: "*Just Book It*!". Secure the returns when the opportunity presents itself. In the volatile world of biotech, waiting for a molecule to get market approval is risky. The odds may seem favourable at times, but the reality is that many molecules fail to clear the final regulatory hurdles.

One of the most reliable exit opportunities in this sector arises when a pharmaceutical company acquires a biotech firm. For investors, this is often a golden exit. When a pharmaceutical partner steps in and buys out a biotech company, it is not only a strong vote of confidence in the company's assets but also a clear signal for investors to exit. At this juncture, the investor has already reaped the financial rewards of the acquisition. Holding on any longer, waiting for the molecule's approval, introduces unnecessary risk. The deal itself is the moment to capitalize on the investment, lock in the gains and move forward.

For my biotech and pharma investments, mergers and acquisitions (M&A) have consistently been the cornerstone of a successful exit strategy in biotech. They represent the most practical and predictable pathway to realizing returns. The logic is simple: when a larger pharmaceutical company acquires a smaller biotech firm, it signifies the culmination of a process. The acquiring company has likely conducted exhaustive due diligence, valuing the biotech company's intellectual property, pipeline, and future potential value. For an investor, this is the biggest validation for a good investment with a clear exit and tangible financial return.

This approach extends beyond biotech and applies equally to medtech companies as well as digital healthcare companies, which operate under similar dynamics.

Promoter buybacks are especially common in the Asian market. Here, the dynamics of control and ownership play a significant role. Many promoters are keen to retain full control of their companies and are reluctant to let ownership shift to third-party strategic investors. For them, a buyback represents a way to consolidate control while providing the investor with a fair exit. From an investor's perspective, this arrangement offers a level of predictability that is often absent in other types of exits. Buybacks also have legal agreements to buy investor shares at a predefined exit rate or with a predefined internal rate of return (IRR).

The nuances of exit strategies, whether through M&A or promoter buybacks, underscore their critical role in determining the success of any biotech investment. As exciting as science and innovation may be, the goal of any investment is to realize returns. A well-planned and carefully executed exit strategy is not just a matter of preference—it is a necessity!

Reflecting on my own portfolio, I see a clear pattern. The investments that have delivered the highest success rates are those where the exit strategy was carefully considered from the outset. Whether it was a biotech company acquired through M&A or a digital healthcare company offering a promoter buyback, the key was having a defined plan. Investing without an exit strategy is like setting sail without a destination—it's a journey bound for uncertainty.

In biotech, this approach is especially crucial because the stakes are so high. The timelines are long, the risks are numerous, and the capital requirements are substantial. It is a field where success hinges not just on the science but on the strategy behind the investment. Understanding when to enter, when to hold, and most importantly, when to exit, is what separates successful investors from the rest.

The lesson I've learned is clear: never get too attached. Invest with your head, not your heart. Define your entry and exit points with precision, and when the time comes to walk away, do so without hesitation. The world of biotech is filled with promise and potential, but it is also rife with uncertainty. The ability to navigate this uncertainty, to remain objective and disciplined, is what ultimately leads to success.

Most pharmaceutical companies that have chosen to invest in emerging markets like India have adopted a strategy that diverges considerably from what one would observe in other parts of the world. India's strength is not just in manufacturing but in unparalleled expertise in process innovation, which is at the core of the country's pharmaceutical landscape and makes it distinct globally. This strength comes from deep chemical expertise coupled with the ability to study a molecule that is "*off-patent*" so that that molecule can be synthesized with speed with innovative process and affordable as a generic compared to the innovator molecule.

While certainly a technical accomplishment, process innovation is really the perfected art only after years of research and understanding of chemistry on an acute plane. It permits Indian pharmaceutical houses to capture this market space for high-quality, affordable, generic versions of critical drugs available at a third of the international price. Perhaps the best place to begin exploring this strategy lies in the case of one of our most noted investments: Matrix Labs.

Based out of Hyderabad, *Matrix Labs*, was one among the many glories of Indian process innovation prowess. It is not just some pharmaceutical manufacturing concern; it's a company whose vision is rather unique and much rooted in effective and cost-saving production of a critical drug component. The synthesis of the active pharmaceutical ingredient (API) for the compound *Celexa* also known as Citalopram remains the claim of fame for the synthesis of this entity.

Citalopram, a molecule used in the production of antidepressant medication, was a lucrative drug, originally developed and patented by innovators who had invested millions in its discovery. When the patent expired, Matrix Labs saw an opportunity. The company's scientists, armed with profound chemical expertise and an innovative mindset, developed a process to synthesize Citalopram more efficiently than anyone else.

What made Matrix's approach so radical was its speed and cost-effectiveness.

They were able not only to reduce the time of production, but also to cut costs by half, creating a product that could compete fiercely in the world market. By the time that the molecule would go off patent, Matrix was ready to descend upon the market with a quality yet cheaper alternative. This made a huge challenge to the original patent holders, giving Matrix an edge hard to ignore. In an intensively competitive business, the company realized that growth had to be multidimensional to really thrive.

To help this along, the firm was ambitious in its inorganic expansion plans. Matrix acquired several smaller pharmaceutical firms that would be strategic in nature, support its existing capabilities and increase its revenue streams. These purchases allowed Matrix to achieve two key goals. First, they strengthened the top line- their revenue. They added new products and markets to their inventory, thus growing their sales volume and expanding the scope of the business. Secondly, they bolstered the bottom line- profitability. The operational efficiency and cost benefits that the group derived from those acquisitions translated to higher margins and strong financials.

Over five years, this strategic process innovation and inorganic growth combination transformed Matrix Labs. What began as a rather small pharmaceutical company became a player in the industry, with revenues of several hundred million dollars. Their success was not ignored.

The turning point came when the prominent American pharmaceutical company, Mylan Pharma, decided to take a bold move. Mylan recognized the huge potential of the Indian pharmaceutical market and saw Matrix as the perfect vehicle to establish a foothold in the subcontinent. In a landmark deal, Mylan acquired Matrix Labs for a staggering 1.1 billion US dollars.

This was a landmark deal for me, as it was my second unicorn exit in the pharmaceutical industry. It was a moment of immense pride and validation for the investment decisions we had made. Watching Matrix's journey, from its humble beginnings to becoming a billion-dollar enterprise, was nothing short of extraordinary.

Beyond Matrix, our investments in India have also ventured into the realm of digital health companies, a domain that sits at the fascinating intersection of information technology and biology. These companies are redefining healthcare by leveraging data and digital tools to enhance patient outcomes and streamline medical processes. While they operate in a different sphere than traditional pharmaceutical companies, their potential for innovation and impact is no less significant.

This sets an important example of the transformative power of process innovation and strategic vision. It is also illustrative of the importance of understanding a market's unique strengths and using them to create value.

In India, the ability to innovate processes—to make them faster, cheaper, and more efficient—has been the cornerstone of success in the pharmaceutical industry. It has been a worthwhile investment for investors to recognize and support this strength, one that continues to mould the healthcare landscape around the world.

India's vast reservoir of talent in Information Technology has emerged as a cornerstone of its transformation across various industries, particularly in healthcare. This deep pool of expertise in coding and algorithm development has proven to be more than just a technical asset—it is a catalyst driving innovation at the interface of medical sciences, data analytics and artificial intelligence. The convergence of these domains has created fertile ground for advancements that are revolutionizing the healthcare landscape.

One area where this fusion is particularly evident is in the realm of medical imaging and signal processing technology. Here, digital health has taken centre stage, offering solutions that were once considered the realm of science fiction. The power of artificial intelligence, when coupled with machine learning and deep learning models, has provided a groundbreaking toolkit for radiographers and medical professionals.

Imagine the painstaking effort it once took to detect tumors, with radiographers relying solely on their trained eyes and traditional imaging techniques. The limitations of human vision meant that certain anomalies remained hidden, buried in layers of complexity. But today, thanks to AI-powered medical imaging and computer vision technology, these invisible threats can be identified with remarkable precision. Algorithms trained on vast datasets analyze images in ways that transcend human capability, detecting even the subtlest irregularities that might otherwise escape notice. It is a transformation that not only enhances diagnostic accuracy but also saves lives by enabling earlier interventions.

India's unique edge in this space stems from its ability to rapidly generate and refine these machine learning and deep learning models. The synergy between cutting-edge technology and a vast, diverse pool of medical data allows Indian innovators to push the boundaries of what is possible. This progress is not just incremental, it is revolutionary, setting the stage for a future where healthcare is more precise, accessible, and efficient.

Another area that is shaping healthcare is Electronic Health records (EHR). This is much more than an electronic version of patient files, representing a paradigm shift in the way medical data is managed, accessed, and utilized. With patient information available in a seamless fashion across multiple providers, care will be uninterrupted, and decisions will be made faster by the healthcare provider.

This makes the record more useful because data flows seamlessly from primary, secondary, and tertiary centres. It reduces redundancies and errors, thereby improving patient outcomes. The dream of the whole medical history of a patient is available at the touch of a button for every doctor that one goes to. This is no longer a dream but a reality that is taking shape globally, thanks to the rise of digital health technologies. The COVID-19 pandemic really served as the catalyst, quickening the progress of telemedicine adoption throughout the country. But before the onset of the COVID-19 outbreak, telemedicine was perceived largely as an additive service—a form of convenience but not a necessary service. And in the world post-COVID, it will be a lifeline, filling and bridging these gaps between multiple levels of delivery.

Telemedicine has been revolutionary in rural areas where, historically, access to specialists and advanced medical facilities has been limited. Today, video consultations and remote monitoring have enabled the most remote parts of the country to access doctors' expertise in metropolitan cities. It has improved accessibility and lightened the load on overcrowded tertiary care centres.

Digital health in all its forms is no doubt one of the most exciting growth areas of healthcare, making it accessible and affordable. Technology meets compassion where innovation is focused on making people's lives better. The investment here is in more than finance-it is investing in a brighter, healthier tomorrow.

As a person who's witnessed both our investments in pharma manufacturing and digital health produce strong returns for many reasons, the two factors stand out prominently: one being that the returns are on top of the curve in learning curve as well as the market curve. With the rapid pace of change today, adapting quickly is crucial for success in this new environment.

In addition to the forward-thinking approach, these businesses have utilized inorganic growth strategies to great effect. By acquiring complementary companies and expanding their capabilities, they have not only strengthened their positions in the market but also mitigated risks. This strategic expansion has allowed them to build robust, scalable models that deliver consistent returns.

Risk management too has been part of their success. With health care as such a dynamic, unpredictable industry, a shrewd business plan is an indispensable part of survival. All our investments were based on comprehensive planning and clearly defined commercialization strategies. And these are plans that maximize returns but, of course, work toward aligning the final output with both what the market wants and long-term goals in the company's vision.

From what I have witnessed, it appears that Asia can be a vanguard for a global healthcare revolution. Its strengths in technical excellence, innovative zest, and access to healthcare have made it uniquely positioned to contribute to the same. The road ahead is quite long, but the journey thus far has already been very promising.

Thanks for being on this transformative journey with me. We're not just investing in businesses here; we are investing in a vision of a healthier, more equitable world through innovation, collaboration, and a relentless focus on the future. And that, to me, is the most rewarding return of all.

Chapter 9 - The Future of Biotech Investments: Trends and Strategic Insights

Biotechnology is the future. It is the only way we are going to be able to feed and fuel the world's growing population."

— Craig Venter

We are on the brink of an era that I confidently describe as the golden phase of the biotech revolution. The term is not to be taken lightly, as evidence of this renaissance can be found all around us, including the seamless integration of cutting-edge technology such as artificial intelligence and the genomic revolution.

Together, these forces are reshaping health care, altering how we diagnose, treat, and eventually care for patients. Let's start with the intersection of artificial intelligence and genomic science.

There lies at their nexus a profound opportunity to redefine health care at the patient level. This is not a theoretical shift but one that has already begun to materialize in tangible, life-altering ways.

Electronic health records (EHRs) and genomic diagnostics are two cornerstones of this transformation. For example, in the past, the pap smear test was the gold standard for early detection of cervical cancer in many women. While undeniably, it was a significant step in its time, the pap smear had its limitations. The stability and a simple procedure: yes, but the tendency for mistakes, flaws that only after time would have a disastrous aftermath, the whole process, revolutionary as it initially was, was far from infallible. Today we stepped into another dimension. DNA-based diagnostics have revolutionized cervical cancer testing. This is not an incremental innovation but rather disruptive. DNA testing for cervical cancer has brought accuracy and reliability to a level that was unattainable previously. The errors and uncertainties that loomed over pap smear results have been dramatically reduced, if not eliminated altogether.

This is the genomic revolution at work—a clear example of how technology can overhaul often long-standing methods and bring results that inspire confidence and save lives. But this is not where the story ends. Breast cancer has also been addressed by the combined knowledge power of artificial intelligence and medical imaging.

Machine learning (ML) models and deep learning (DL) algorithms bring a capability that is as remarkable as it is revolutionary. These models are trained to analyse images with a precision far beyond human capacity, identifying tumours that would otherwise remain invisible to the naked eye.

The implications for this advancement are profound. Screening for breast cancer, once a challenging and often imprecise endeavour, is now more accurate, efficient, and accessible. The role of artificial intelligence in this space cannot be overstated. It is an assistant to healthcare providers, but it also becomes a partner in a new revolution in the detection and treatment of breast cancer.

Thus, here's a look at the grand vision of how health care in the future shall look as supported by three basic pillars: *personalization*, *prevention*, and *product development.* These paradigms on its own merge with each other as well to deliver the whole solution.

This would mean that personalized medicine is, in the ultimate sense, treating the person, not the disease. It is a belief that every patient's genetic composition, lifestyle, or environmental influences play a highly important role in defining their health and well-being.

Just a few decades back, this type of personalization would have been considered impossible, but due to progress in genomics and AI, it is now achievable.

Preventive medicine, on the other hand, is about shifting focus from treatment to prevention. It is about identifying risks before they manifest as illnesses, allowing interventions to be made at a stage when they are most effective. This approach not only saves lives but also reduces the burden on healthcare systems, making them more sustainable in the long run.

Finally, there is product-based medicine, an area that feeds from innovation and intellectual property. Patent commercialization in the biotech industry is the best example of this.

Each new product drug, a diagnostic tool, or a therapeutic device would represent one step forward in our fight against diseases and their effective management to improve patient outcomes.

Intellectual property is not just a legal construct here; it is the backbone of an industry that relies on creativity and innovation to push boundaries.

Perhaps what is even more fascinating about this revolution is its genomic side. While genomics diagnostics have started showing impact in so many places, it would seem to reach further than simple diagnosis. It seems to enter prognostics: predicting how the disease would probably unfold, hence making interventions targeted. In such a future world, diagnostic ability becomes much more comprehensive in its predictions.

This brings us to the "wellness" industry, which I believe will soon outpace the "illness" industry in scale and importance. Wellness is not the absence of disease; it is a holistic state of physical, mental, and emotional health.

Nowadays the use of wearables such as smart watches and access to smart phones has become prevalent amongst consumers. These smart devices have the power to collect data regarding the individual lifestyle of a person and monitor various health metrics such as sleep cycle, sedentary lifestyle, and food habits measuring the calorific value of the food consumed daily. Data collected from such smart devices are now crunched and annotated to determine "health span and longevity of a human being". Genomic insights will play a pivotal role here, enabling personalized wellness plans that cater to individual needs and preferences. The future of biotech investments lies in embracing these shifts and recognizing the infinite potential they hold in anti-ageing and healthy living (longevity). It's not just the number of years a person lives that is important but also the quality of lifespan. This golden phase is not some moment in time but a foundation on which we can create a healthier, more equitable future. The integration of artificial intelligence with genomics is not merely a technological advancement; it is a revolution in our ability to perceive and understand healthcare.

In this journey toward transformation, it is not so much a time of watching events unfold but rather creating new ones.

Investing in all these technologies with the emphasis placed on the right culture and incentives for innovation to lay down the ground for healthcare cantered on patients are only some of the promises the biotech revolution comes with. The promise of which holds within its power to remake our world altogether.

There is, of course, more than just treatment of illness in the future of healthcare; it's fundamentally about fostering wellness. This brings about a radical shift in the meaning of health itself.

The healthcare system will no longer wait for the emergence of disease symptoms but rather look forward to risk prediction and action to preserve good health. Imagine a world where tests for predicting the development of chronic conditions such as diabetes, strokes, or heart attacks abound. The possibilities are now identified using deep learning models with a good degree of accuracy. Advanced tools analyse data in ways that have never been imaginable before, showing a roadmap on how an individual might be predisposed to some health conditions.

This predictive capability offers the possibility for timely interventions with patients, giving them the ability to take steps that can enormously reduce their risk. These mitigating factors could be lifestyle changes, dietary adjustments, preventive medications, or therapies. The principle is simple and revolutionary: *If the root causes of diseases are diagnosed early, then health outcomes can be drastically improved.*

This revolution in healthcare has far-reaching effects that go beyond an individual; it can change whole society, making way for "population screening" more of a reality!

Health Insurance:

One of the industries that will undergo a sea change is health insurance. Health insurance has, until now, operated on a very broad, generalized model. In other words, it's been a one-size-fits-all model. This has resulted in inefficiencies and a lack of personalization in addressing individual health needs. The future promises much more.

As genomics and data science continue to advance, they will increasingly intersect with healthcare. Personalized health insurance models are one such possible outcome and inevitable for the future of personalised healthcare.

These models account for an individual's genotype and phenotype, in addition to lifestyles, stress, and even lifestyle habits. Insurance premiums will cease to be uniformly charged but now will be differential, reflecting every individual's respective risk profile.

For instance, a physically active subject with low genetically predisposed chances of certain conditions may pay less than a highly sedentary character with higher hereditary risk elements.

Without the strides that digital health is making, such personalization would be impossible. This ever-evolving area allows us to track and know lifestyle habits at an unprecedented level of granularity.

As mentioned earlier, smartphones and smartwatches have become ubiquitous devices, gathering an immense amount of information about the user. Such devices monitor sleep patterns, activity levels, heart rate, and more. The data generated is then harnessed and analysed, feeding into sophisticated models that predict health risks and provide insights into an individual's overall lifestyle. Singapore-based *AktivoLabs* is partnering with various insurance companies and revolutionizing the health insurance business models with the help of its proprietary risk-based predictive "Aktivoscore".

These technologies make the practice of medicine so deeply personal that a care provider can help the patient know he is getting ample sleep, engaging in enough lifestyle activities, or how one can take control of dealing with stress to enhance his way of living. And that's much beyond just addressing disease; they enable individuals to live healthier lives and live the best they can do.

Now, let's turn to the biotech side of this revolution, where the future is more promising despite the high stakes. The biotech industry is facing rising costs and long timelines for developing new therapies. It takes billions of dollars and years of intense research and clinical trials to bring a New Chemical Entity (NCE) to the market. This is not only expensive but also risky in terms of its success rates as the failure in drug development is high. AI couple with Quantum Innovation, promises to be a game-changer in drug discovery and development.

Using AI and Quantum Innovation, one hopes to save time and costs associated with the processes. Together bot AI and Quantum have the capacity to analyze large datasets, spot patterns, and predict outcomes-abilities that are very helpful in finding new drug candidates.

For example, AI-driven models can sort through millions of compounds to find those most likely to succeed as drug candidates. This targeted approach increases the hit rate of finding viable treatments, making the drug development pipeline more efficient.

Moreover, these models can simulate how potential drugs might interact with specific targets in the body, helping researchers refine their approaches before clinical trials even begin.

The main areas that need to be developed in the sector include those addressing cancer, mental health, and chronic diseases. Such issues have for a long time remained inapplicable with a straightforward solution.

AI incorporation into biotech research presents a new way forward, thus opening avenues that were hitherto inaccessible, unearthing novel therapies, and giving way to treatments that are more efficient and targeted.

Yet, in this landscape lies some of the promise of risks associated with drug discovery and development. It remains an activity rife with failures and setbacks. Nonetheless, infusion into this area promises hope. Streamlined research processes, as well as the improved predictive accuracy AI promises, reduce failure chances and quicken the pace of development from the lab to the market.

This is not just an incremental step but a paradigm shift. It is a move toward a future where the boundaries of what is possible in healthcare are continually expanded. A future where wellness is prioritized over illness, where health insurance is as personalized as the care it supports, and where groundbreaking therapies emerge faster and more reliably than ever before.

Artificial intelligence and machine learning, digital health, and biotechnology converge to create a backbone of healthcare, within a new paradigm of healthcare delivery.

Instead of taking turns in an isolated manner, they work together and quite synergistically, one amplifying the other, to create a future for healthcare wherein people are not surviving but thriving.

For sure, as we go through this revolution, it is important to observe that the path ahead is one of great promise and equally huge complexity. The challenges are as significant as the opportunities, which demand careful navigation, collaboration, and innovation. But if there is something sure, it is this: the future of healthcare is bright, and its foundation is being laid today.

Green Chemistry & Sustainable Innovation:

The pharmaceutical industry is transforming itself to keep pace with green chemistry. The pharma of tomorrow will see the sustainability of practice and innovations as redefining the very face of a greener tomorrow, one in which environmental awareness becomes a compulsion rather than just an ideal.

These changes are driven by a commitment to reducing the environmental footprint of the industry, whether mitigating noise pollution, curbing air contamination, or treating water pollution caused by effluents released during the drug synthesis process. This movement towards sustainability is a deliberate effort to create an industry that harmonizes with nature rather than exploiting it.

It is not just about compliance with regulations or meeting public opinion; it is about embracing a vision of net-zero carbon neutrality. Achieving such a goal demands an intricate balance of science, innovation, and responsibility.

The path forward involves implementing robust frameworks and innovative tools that can measure and manage the impact of pharmaceutical manufacturing on the environment. This journey to *net-zero sustainability* is not some vague, distant objective; rather, it provides the very framework on which the industry will change. Every move, every set of frameworks, and every policy created can fundamentally transform the process of pharmaceutical manufacturing.

The implications are that, beyond becoming an industry that leaves less of an ecological footprint, this industry will fundamentally shift in its social role. The pharmaceutical sector is bound to lead the revolution because the pharmaceutical industry is natively adaptable in nature.

Since its inception, this industry thrived on evolvability responding to some global health issues or adapting scientific advancements. Such adaptability, now, targets pressing global issues such as climate change.

The recent international conferences, for example, the COP meetings held in Europe and the Middle East, have made environmental challenges look even more pressing.

These meetings have acted as wake-up calls that point out such issues as depletion of the ozone layer, depletion of natural resources, and accelerated impacts of climate change.

Pharmaceutical industries, like any other, cannot remain aloof from these facts. If anything, it has a greater responsibility to act given its potential to make a significant difference through sustainable innovative practices. Climate change is something that needs more than just acknowledgement; it requires action.

In the pharmaceutical sector, this involves reimagining manufacturing processes, adopting innovative tools, and creating models that consider the stewardship of the environment. The push for greener practices does not stop at reducing emissions or managing waste; it goes all the way to the heart of drug discovery and development. One striking example of this shift is the adoption of *organoids in drug discovery*. These are organ-like structures that mimic the function and complexity of human organs on a smaller scale.

Organoids represent a groundbreaking alternative to traditional animal testing, which has long been a cornerstone of pharmaceutical research. Traditional drug testing relies heavily on animal models, from small rodents like rats and mice to larger animals like rabbits and even chimpanzees.

Although these methods have provided invaluable insights, they come with a significant ethical and environmental cost. The lives of countless animals are sacrificed in the name of progress, and the ecological toll of maintaining such models is far from negligible.

Organoids are the sustainable solution to this dilemma. These structures allow researchers to study the effects of drugs on human-like tissues without the need for live animals. The complex interactions within the human body are replicated by organoids, which provide more accurate and predictive data than traditional models.

This not only accelerates the pace of drug discovery but also reduces the environmental and ethical burdens associated with animal testing.

Organoids rise, emblematic of the new wave in non-conventional models of pharmaceutical research. The tools here are testaments to a pharmaceutical industry with a focus on sustainability and innovation. Through such actions, the pharmaceutical sector advances science but also acts as a prime example for the rest of the industry to emulate.

The future of the pharmaceutical industry is at the nexus of green chemistry, sustainability, and innovation.

It is a future where the progress of the pharmaceutical industry will not be defined by new drugs developed or profits earned but by the positive impact on the planet.

Every step taken towards greener practices, every organoid used in place of an animal model, and every framework implemented to reduce emissions is a step toward a healthier world—for humans and the environment alike.

As the industry looks to the future, the challenge is as great as the opportunity. The path to net-zero carbon neutrality is complex and demanding, requiring cooperation, perseverance, and a willingness to rethink established ways of doing things. And yet, the potential rewards—to the industry and to the planet—make this journey not only worthwhile but necessary. Many pharmaceutical companies have made net zero commitments, such as GSK, committing to become completely net zero by 2045. Amongst other announced initiatives, the company is starting an R&D programme to find an alternative, greener propellant for their rescue inhalers, with 55% of GSK's total climate impact coming from patient use of these inhalers. If successful, the project could reduce the environmental impact of rescue inhalers by 90%.

Pfizer has set a goal to decrease its greenhouse gas (GHG) emissions by 95%, and value chain emissions by 90%, from 2019 levels, by 2040. The company plans to do this with renewable energy investments, aiding suppliers to set science-based emission reduction goals, and reducing emissions related to upstream logistics and business travel.

However, companies need to focus on initiatives to reduce Scope 3 emissions, which is where most emissions lie. This is a shared responsibility between pharmaceutical companies and the supply chain, but essential if companies are going to meet net zero targets.

In the pharmaceutical industry, sustainability is not a peripheral matter anymore; rather, it serves as the ground on which tomorrow is being shaped. This will not only allow the problems of today to be addressed but also provide a world for healthcare and care for the environment to go in tandem.

"Novel & Affordable" Cancer Therapy:

The world is amid a revolutionary transition in the war against chronic diseases. Such remarkable medical science advancement has taken centre stage within cell therapy, T-cell therapy, gene therapy, and other high-profile techniques such as RNA therapeutics. Indeed, these progressions are no incremental steps, but rather gargantuan leaps for mankind to get out of the puzzle of chronic diseases, particularly one of the world's most persistent health problems- cancer.

Take *CAR T-cell therapy*, for example—Chimeric Antigen Receptor T-Cell therapy is a transformative technique that has captured the imagination of researchers and clinicians alike. This highly specialized form of immunotherapy is designed to harness the power of the body's own immune system to combat cancer cells. Through the reprogramming of a patient's T-cells to recognize and attack specific cancer cells, CAR T-cell therapy represents a beacon of hope for chronic cancer cases that were once deemed untreatable.

The real revolution, however, is not only in developing such therapies but in making them affordable and accessible. It is in this respect that countries like India are trying to carve out an identity in the global healthcare map. Traditionally, CAR T-cell treatments and advanced therapies have been so expensive that they remained out of the reach of millions.

In the West, the price of a single CAR T-cell therapy can go upto $500,000 making it a luxury that only a few people can afford. India is rewriting that narrative through a powerful focus on affordable innovation. Cutting-edge CAR-T cancer therapy, called NexCAR19 is now made available in India at one-tenth the cost. NexCAR19 raises hope that this transformative class of medicine will become readily available in low-and middle-income countries. The vision: democratize cutting-edge health care by bringing costs down without lowering quality or effectiveness.

Imagine a world where a treatment, which might be expensive to the tune of millions of dollars in the West, is available for a fraction of that amount in India. This is no far-fetched dream but a reality that is being moulded by the robust investment of the country in the sphere of research and development.

Indian scientists, armed with ingenuity and a relentless drive to make healthcare equitable, are leading the charge in redefining how advanced therapies are developed and delivered.

The impact of affordable innovation is profound. For a cancer patient fighting through chronic illness, the difference in receiving treatment often comes down to affordability. Thus, by pricing CAR T-cell therapy at about one-tenth of that in the West, India is saving lives as well as opening a future standard for world healthcare.

However, these efforts do come with difficulties. It is a tough balancing act between scientific integrity, technological competence, and economic feasibility to come up with cost-effective solutions.

It involves rethinking the entire healthcare value chain, from research to manufacturing, distribution, to delivery. Effective collaborations are also required among academia, industry, and government, and knowledge of the distinct health needs of the people within the region.

The approach of India to affordable innovation is based on a recognition of its dual responsibility: to contribute to the global advancement of medical science while addressing the healthcare disparities within its own borders. The country's vast and diverse population provides a unique testing ground for scaling therapies that are not only effective but also accessible to patients from varied socioeconomic backgrounds.

This commitment to affordability does not mean cutting corners or compromising the integrity of science.

On the contrary, it is about finding innovative ways to optimize resources, streamline processes, and leverage indigenous capabilities to achieve world-class outcomes.

Researchers prove that excellence and affordability are not mutually exclusive but can coexist harmoniously.

Considering this might further propagate the phenomenon. Innovation in the treatment of CAR T-cell also could change international healthcare dynamics drastically.

It brings the message among the other country systems to revolutionize their methodology on pricing access. It refutes the misconception that advanced medicinal facilities must eventually add to the massive expense.

For India, the stakes are both personal and global. On one hand, the country is addressing the pressing healthcare needs of its own citizens, where chronic diseases like cancer are becoming increasingly prevalent.

On the other hand, it is positioning itself as a global leader in affordable innovation, offering solutions that could transform the way chronic diseases are managed worldwide.

The story of India's role in the fight against chronic diseases is one of hope, resilience, and ingenuity. It is a testament to what can be achieved when a nation dares to think differently and prioritize humanity over profit. It is a narrative that challenges the status quo and paves the way for a future where no patient is denied life-saving treatment simply because they cannot afford it.

The advances in cell therapy, T-cell therapy, gene therapy, and CAR T-cell therapy are not just milestones in medical science; they are harbingers of a new era in healthcare. They embody the spirit of innovation and the relentless pursuit of solutions that address not only the disease but also the systemic barriers that prevent access to care.

This reminds India of the affordable innovation journey; it shows that progress is not just technological but the ability to make the technology accessible to everyone. This becomes a call for the global health community to consider equity and inclusion, sharing benefits from science around the world.

As the world struggles with the weight of chronic diseases, the promise of affordable innovation shines brighter than ever. It is a promise that transcends borders, holding hope for millions and reiterating the fact that healthcare is a right, not a privilege. In this journey, India is not only a participant but a trailblazer, redefining what is possible and inspiring others to follow.

There lies an arduous road ahead. The message, however, is loud and clear.

Investment in *affordable innovation* helps India move a step further into addressing urgent population needs even while contributing towards an international wave for the sake of transforming health into a powerful tool for change.

A journey requires nothing but valour, collaboration, and an all-encompassing, unwavering commitment towards equity and inclusive ends.

But if the breakthroughs in CAR T-cell therapy and other innovations are any guide, it is a journey worth taking—one that promises to change lives and leave an indelible mark on the future of healthcare.

Investment in the Biotechnology Sector:

The biotechnology sector continues to captivate venture capital (VC) and private equity (PE) investors, offering transformative potential in healthcare through cutting-edge platforms and innovative therapies. The landscape of biotech investment has evolved dramatically over the last decade. The COVID-19 pandemic underscored the sector's critical role in addressing global health emergencies, driving a surge in VC and PE activity. Post-pandemic, however, investment patterns have normalized, shifting toward fewer but larger deals focused on late-stage ventures with validated clinical pathways. This selective approach reflects a broader trend toward de-risking investments, as highlighted in PitchBook analysis.

Despite a reduction in deal count, the sector remains a strong draw for substantial capital. Life sciences VC funding accounted for approximately 65% of healthcare deal values in 2024, underlining the resource-intensive nature of biotech innovation Mature companies ready for commercialization are increasingly favoured over early-stage startups, signalling a shift in investor priorities.

The pivot toward late-stage investments reflects a strategic focus on scalability and revenue generation. Mature companies with robust clinical data and defined commercialization strategies are attracting investor interest, mitigating risks associated with early-stage ventures. This trend is exemplified by the growth in Series A rounds, with average capital rounds climbing from $50 million to nearly $100 million. This shift underscores the escalating capital requirements in biotech development.

The biopharmaceutical landscape is witnessing a surge in M&A activity, with leading firms leveraging acquisitions to consolidate expertise and expand their technological capabilities. High-profile transactions, such as Johnson & Johnson's acquisition of Intra-Cellular Therapies, illustrate the growing trend toward strategic consolidation.

Emerging markets in Southeast Asia and Latin America are increasingly appealing to investors due to their cost advantages and untapped talent pools. These regions are set to play a pivotal role in both research and manufacturing operations.

The biotech investment landscape is not without challenges. Rising R&D costs, intricate regulatory landscapes, and macroeconomic fluctuations, such as varying interest rates, pose significant hurdles. Additionally, the persistent valuation gap between public and private markets complicates exit strategies for investors. Exit opportunities are further constrained by decreasing federal interest rates, delaying IPOs for pre-clinical biopharma players to avoid valuation cuts.

Nevertheless, recent developments suggest a softening in the exit market, with IPO-ready companies such as *Spring Health, Omada Health, and Sword Health* generating significant investor interest. The adoption of hub-and-spoke exit strategies for AI pharma companies is expected to further enhance exit viability.

The sector's resilience and innovative potential remain strong. By concentrating on fewer but larger investments, alongside a focus on scalable platforms and exploring opportunities in diverse geographic regions, biotechnology firmly establishes itself as a foundational pillar in advancing healthcare innovation.

New technological trends will shape the future of investments, starting with Artificial Intelligence (AI), which is revolutionizing biotechnology, particularly in drug discovery and clinical trial optimization. By embedding AI into R&D workflows, firms can significantly reduce timelines while enhancing success probabilities. Noteworthy partnerships, such as AstraZeneca's collaboration with *BenevolentAI*, exemplify how AI is being harnessed to identify innovative therapeutic targets.

However, the journey of AI in biotech has been challenging. Lengthy drug development cycles and limited success from early implementations have tempered initial optimism. While platforms such as AstraZeneca's collaboration offer promising results, overall outcomes have yet to meet expectations. Recent shifts toward biologics-focused generative AI (GenAI) platforms signal potential breakthroughs, though these advancements must navigate complex regulatory landscapes. For instance, California's restrictive AI regulations contrast sharply with the European Union's comprehensive AI governance, which may provide a standardization blueprint.

Platform based technologies, including ML-enabled drug discovery and cell therapies, are increasingly prioritized for their scalability and broad applicability across multiple therapeutic domains. Recent funding rounds highlight this enthusiasm, with *Umoja Biopharma* raising $100 million, *Tune Therapeutics* securing $175 million, and *Be Biopharma* obtaining $92 million. Additionally, *ElevateBio's* leadership in biopharma services demonstrates sustained interest in platform-based innovation.

Recognizing the complexities of in-house AI development, biopharma firms are embracing strategic partnerships with AI-focused companies. These collaborations provide access to advanced technologies while allowing firms to concentrate on their core scientific competencies. The emergence of AI service models reflects a strategic pivot, enabling firms to capitalize on AI-driven efficiencies without overextending internal resources.

Focus will also be important towards advances in genomics and personalized medicine, as they are reshaping diagnostics and treatments, especially in oncology and rare diseases. These technologies offer unprecedented opportunities for tailored therapeutic interventions.

It is also important to note that addressing gaps in women's health is both a moral imperative and a lucrative investment avenue. Areas such as endometriosis and sex-specific treatments are gaining traction, with companies seeking to bridge health disparities and unlock significant market potential.

The future of biotechnology investments hinges on precision and adaptability—prioritizing scalable platforms, leveraging AI, and addressing underserved markets such as women's health. As the industry evolves, investors who align with these trends and navigate the sector's inherent complexities will be positioned to foster transformative advancements and secure robust returns. By striking a balance between innovation and risk management, biotechnology is poised to redefine the boundaries of medicine and deliver profound global health benefits.

Chapter 10: The Impact of AI on Healthcare

"AI is perhaps the most transformational technology of our time, and healthcare is perhaps AI's most pressing application."

- Satya Nadella, CEO Microsoft Inc USA

At a rate I have never seen before, Artificial Intelligence (AI) is transforming healthcare by bringing about breakthroughs that will completely change medical research, diagnosis, and patient care. Healthcare decisions are no longer based solely on experience and gut feeling. With AI, healthcare is becoming a data-driven field, where precision medicine, predictive analytics, and intelligent automation are playing the lead role.

Due to leaders' and governments' recognition of AI's potential, its adoption in healthcare is accelerating globally. At the AI Action Summit in Paris, Indian Prime Minister Narendra Modi emphasized the importance of developing user-friendly AI solutions that prioritize patient safety and well-being. He emphasized the importance of creating ethical AI systems and the need for AI algorithms to be inclusive and transparent. Bias is among the most urgent problems with AI in healthcare. Some people may be disproportionately affected by recommendations for unequal treatment made by artificial intelligence algorithms trained on unrepresentative data. To tackle this, increasingly there is an open-source campaign for AI models that can be audited and improved to eliminate biases, creating equitable and equal healthcare for all.

The global AI in the healthcare market demonstrates rapid expansion at present. For the current year market valuation amounts to $19.27 billion but projections indicate that the healthcare AI sector will expand by 38.5% annually from 2024 through 2030 thus reshaping healthcare delivery methods. Hospitals alongside research facilities continue to increase their investments in AI solutions since 79% of healthcare organizations have integrated AI into their operations.

Healthcare organizations achieve their desired improvements through the widespread adoption of AI because they want to enhance efficiency while saving costs and delivering better patient results. The deployment of AI technology generates significant financial returns because every dollar spent on its implementation leads to predicted revenue of $3.70. Hospitals along with healthcare providers rapidly implement AI systems because of the exceptional ROI achievement.

The influence of AI on clinical decision-making is significant. Doctors are now utilizing AI-driven diagnostic systems that are able can identify diseases with previously unimaginable precision. AI models, which are trained on vast medical databases, can pick up on patterns that would not be caught by human physicians, resulting in earlier and more precise diagnoses.

For example, AI programs reviewing radiology images can identify cancers at early stages with accuracy that matches or exceeds that of seasoned radiologists. This technology is not intended to replace physicians but to enhance their skill set, giving them greater capabilities in making better decisions.

Here is an example of a patient, Michelle Thompson, a 45-year-old female with a medical history of chronic migraines, enters a clinic. Previously, she would be subjected to various tests, see several specialists, and receive trial-and-error prescriptions. But in current times with AI-powered healthcare, her medical history, genes, and lifestyle information can be processed by generative AI, generating a highly precise diagnosis and personalized treatment regime within hours.

The AI system recognizes patterns in her symptoms, cross-references millions of medical cases, and suggests the most effective medication based on her unique physiological response. This is not a futuristic vision, but a present-day reality made possible by AI's integration into healthcare.

Medical imaging diagnosis stands as one of the healthcare fields where AI makes fundamental changes through its quick and precise disease identification process. Every day radiologists need to analyze thousands of images to locate abnormalities while their diagnosis performance depends heavily on their imaging interpretation skill. Advanced tools equipped with artificial intelligence enable quick condition identification of tumours together with fractures along with organ abnormalities. Real-time alerts about possibly fatal conditions originate from AI-supported systems developed by *Aidoc* and similar firms which assist radiologists.

The implementation of new technologies maintains high diagnostic accuracy and creates additional efficiency for radiologists who can allocate their time to handle complex medical situations and treat patients. The detection of cancer cells becomes essential with AI-based screening methods since these technologies identify malignancies during their earliest stages which lead to improved patient survival outcomes.

AI is transforming *mental health* treatment by making it possible to monitor patients continuously and use predictive modelling, thereby enabling early intervention and tailored treatment. Conventional mental health testing usually involves periodic checks, but now AI-based tools are capable of monitoring physiological and behavioural markers in real-time. Wearables and mobile apps read physiological and behavioural signals like heart rate variability, sleep patterns, and social engagement metrics and offer insights into a patient's mental health.

With predictive analytics based on AI, medical practitioners can determine the possibility of developing chronic diseases such as cardiovascular disease and diabetes, which usually carry psychological consequences. Through such insights, individuals have the power to make *proactive lifestyle choices* and receive preventive treatments before complicated health complications can develop. By combining AI with wearable health devices, doctors can monitor patients remotely, identifying anomalies that would otherwise become serious health issues. This strategy moves healthcare from reactive to proactive, enhancing patient outcomes and decreasing hospitalization.

AI is being utilized in robotic-assisted surgeries, where accuracy and minimal invasiveness are paramount. These robot systems powered by AI help surgeons conduct intricate surgeries with higher precision and lower risks, resulting in quicker recovery rates for patients.

Deep learning algorithms used in AI systems detect patterns in CT scans MRIs and X-rays which human vision often fails to see.

The impact of AI in healthcare is further amplified by its ability to analyze massive amounts of patient data in real time, enabling *predictive analytics* for disease prevention. AI models can assess risk factors, detect early symptoms, and predict disease progression, allowing for proactive medical interventions.

For instance, predictive analytics software infused with AI is being utilized to predict the chances of developing chronic conditions like diabetes and cardiovascular disease, leading to premature lifestyle changes and preventive therapies.

By integrating AI with wearable medical devices, physicians can remotely monitor patients and identify irregularities before they become full-blown diseases. This preventative strategy not only enhances patient results but also lowers healthcare expenses on delayed-stage care and hospitalization.

AI-driven clinical decision support systems are supporting disease diagnosis and medical decision-making. AI programs instructed with huge data sets of health records, test results, and imaging studies are capable of recognizing disease with as much accuracy as, or better than, human experts. An AI system designed at Stanford University could identify skin cancer with as much skill as seasoned dermatologists.

The computer model, after being trained on thousands of images of skin, can distinguish between cancerous and benign lesions, offering an extra layer of assurance for physicians when they make a diagnostic decision.

Likewise, in Denmark, researchers have tried out an AI software that identifies cardiac arrests within emergency calls at a 93% success rate compared to 73% for human dispatchers. These examples highlight AI's potential in enhancing diagnostic precision, reducing diagnostic errors, and speeding up treatment initiation.

Major drivers for AI in healthcare: The use of *AI in medicine* is driven by several major drivers, the first being the growing need for efficiency, accuracy, and better patient outcomes. The conventional healthcare system often clogged with lengthy waiting times, overworked doctors and nurses, and errors in diagnosis and treatment through human fallibility, is being redefined by AI-facilitated solutions that digitize operations and speed up decision-making.

AI-powered automation is reducing administrative workloads on healthcare providers so that they can concentrate more on treating patients than filling forms. From controlling electronic health records to streamlining hospital logistics, AI is becoming an indispensable ally in making healthcare operations smoother.

The other primary driver of AI adoption is the *convergence* of big data, the Internet of Things (IoT), and cloud computing in the healthcare sector. The volume of medical information produced every day is too much for human analysis, but AI algorithms can handle enormous amounts of data in real-time, recognizing patterns, forecasting disease outbreaks, and aiding in clinical decision-making.

Wearable health devices, intelligent sensors, and networked medical equipment are constantly gathering patient information, which AI systems scan to give early alerts of impending health problems. These proactive healthcare measures ensure timely intervention, minimizing hospital stays and better patient outcomes.

The automation powers of AI are also helping to simplify hospital processes and patient care. AI chatbots and virtual assistants are lightening the load on healthcare call centres by effectively managing patient queries, appointment scheduling, and even offering initial medical guidance. This not only improves the patient's experience but also maximizes hospital resource utilization.

Aside from direct patient treatment, AI is transforming *medical research and drug development*. Historically, drug discovery has been a time- and money-consuming process, with years passing before a new drug is introduced to the market. AI-based drug discovery platforms are significantly shortening this timeframe by examining large datasets, finding potential drug candidates, and forecasting their efficacy with structural biology experts. This speed in drug development is not only saving lives but also lowering the economic burden on pharmaceutical firms and healthcare systems.

As AI continues to redefine the healthcare sector, attention should still be focused on utilizing its potential to optimize patient outcomes, increase efficiency, and bring healthcare closer to people at reduced costs. The path to AI-enabled healthcare is ongoing, but its effects are already being felt in the lives that it is changing. Whether intelligent diagnostics, customized treatment protocols, or operational efficiency, AI has the potential to redefine the future of medicine, bringing high-quality healthcare to all.

The advanced technology of AI continues its focus on two key areas: *personalized treatment* and *mental healthcare* through individual patient data-driven solutions. AI is driving away from traditional one-fits-all medical choices since it analyses genetics alongside lifestyle choices and health backgrounds for creating customized treatment recommendations. AI technology leads to advancements in mental health diagnosis by making both the timing and precision of identification much better.

AI is transforming mental health care by providing innovative solutions for diagnosis, treatment, and patient support. Traditional mental health assessments rely on self-reported symptoms and clinical observations, which can sometimes be subjective and delayed.

AI-powered tools, however, offer real-time, data-driven insights that enhance early detection and personalized treatment.

One of the most promising applications of AI in mental health is early diagnosis. AI models analyse speech patterns, facial expressions, and behavioural data to detect signs of anxiety, depression, and other disorders.

For example, London-based *Thymia* uses AI-powered video games to assess cognitive and emotional responses, helping clinicians identify mental health conditions more accurately. They use this game to analyse mental health problems through a combination of verbal expression together with facial emotional responses and conduct patterns. AI helps healthcare staff monitor patient treatment results which guides clinical decisions about therapy changes.

Patients receive optimal interventions promptly with this technology which decreases error rates in diagnoses as well as ineffectual therapies. Furthermore, AI-based therapy chatbots and virtual counsellors are offering round-the-clock support, ensuring greater access to mental healthcare for individuals who may not have easy access to professional services.

Similarly, AI chatbots like *Woebot* and *Wysa* provide immediate emotional support and cognitive behavioural therapy (CBT) techniques, making mental health resources more accessible.

In addition to individual care, AI is streamlining mental health services at a broader level. AI-powered virtual assistants reduce the burden on healthcare professionals by automating administrative tasks like appointment scheduling and patient follow-ups. This improves efficiency and allows therapists to focus on providing high-quality care.

Despite its benefits, AI in mental health faces challenges, such as data privacy concerns and the need for diverse datasets to minimize biases. However, with continuous advancements and ethical AI development, AI has the potential to revolutionize mental health care, making it more accessible, personalized, and effective worldwide.

AI-powered *virtual nursing assistants* are revolutionizing patient monitoring and engagement, especially in-home care and chronic disease management. With increasing healthcare professional shortages, AI-powered virtual nurses fill the gap by providing real-time reminders, support, and wellness checks.

Care Angel, for example, has built an AI virtual nurse that converses with patients either through voice or text messages, tracking the condition of patients, reminding them when to take medicine, and providing answers to health-related questions.

It is especially valuable to elderly and chronically ill patients who are under constant care but might not have in-person access to the physician at times. With the use of AI for patient interaction, hospital readmissions can be avoided, medication can be taken as prescribed, and timely interventions in the event of health decline can be provided.

AI-driven chatbots and virtual health assistants are also being incorporated into telemedicine platforms, facilitating seamless communication between doctors and patients, and alleviating the workload from human medical professionals.

Despite all the vast opportunities that it carries, AI implementation in healthcare does have challenges. There are the issues of ethics, privacy, and strong regulations. There needs to be clarity about AI models being transparent, explainable, and unbiased. These are very critical in securing the confidence of not only health workers but also patients. In addition, there is an urgent need for ongoing monitoring and verification of AI systems to establish their reliability and efficacy in actual healthcare environments.

As AI continues to gain traction in healthcare, its potential to revolutionize medical practice becomes increasingly apparent. From improving diagnostic accuracy to individualized treatment, AI is enhancing the efficiency, accessibility, and quality of patient care. But with the adoption of AI in healthcare comes ethical and regulatory concerns. Ensuring transparency, minimizing biases in AI models, and patient data privacy are fundamental challenges that need to be met to build trust and promote large-scale adoption.

Despite these challenges, the incorporation of AI in healthcare is full of promise, and as technology continues to advance, its applications will only grow further, making healthcare more efficient, personalized, and patient-centric.

The power of artificial intelligence continuously transforms medical drug research along with hospital administrative functions and medical discovery work. New drug development through traditional methods stretches to over ten years because it demands substantial research time followed by preclinical evaluation and multiple clinical trial phases.

The analysis of large datasets and drug interaction predictions and promising compound identification capabilities allow AI technology to decrease the discovery process from multiple decades to a substantially faster timespan than human researchers work independently. Anticipated drug discovery times get shortened by AI startups who partner up with leading pharmaceutical firms.

Insilico Medicine together with *BenevolentAI* use machine learning algorithms which help their teams identify potential new drugs through much faster discovery rates. By transferring some tasks through this shift researchers can devote more time to perfecting promising compounds instead of performing extensive trial-and-error testing.

Medical research benefits substantially from AI through data processing of massive genomic clinical and molecular datasets. The analysis performed by AI systems discovers patterns which ordinary human analysis cannot complete over a decade's time which leads to increased therapeutic accuracy. The healthcare solution provider *Tempus Labs* incorporates AI technology to read genetic markers which generates customized cancer treatment protocols for patients.

The approach to future medicine with precision by delivering customized treatments to each patient without deploying generic treatments in a mass-market manner. Modern computing speed enabled by AI operates on immense data volumes in real-time to foster discoveries in targeted medical therapeutics which guide doctors toward better clinical results.

The power of artificial intelligence continuously transforms medical drug research along with hospital administrative functions and medical discovery work. New drug development through traditional methods stretches to over ten years because it demands substantial research time followed by preclinical evaluation and multiple clinical trial phases. The analysis of large datasets and drug interaction predictions and promising compound identification capabilities allow AI technology to decrease the discovery process from multiple decades to a substantially faster timespan than human researchers work independently.

Another key field where AI is having a presence is *fraud detection and cybersecurity*. Insurance companies and hospitals are regularly targeted by fake claims, which result in heavy financial losses. AI-based fraud detection systems utilize machine learning algorithms to detect anomalies in hospital billing and insurance claims.

By scanning historical records and identifying suspicious trends, AI can identify potentially fraudulent activities in real time, allowing organizations to respond quickly to rectify situations. AI also enhances cybersecurity by identifying illegal access to medical records and protecting sensitive patient information from cyber-attacks. With healthcare organizations increasingly going digital with their records, AI-powered security solutions are now an indispensable tool in the protection of sensitive information.

Hospital functions are also changing with AI-based automation. Standard administrative procedures that once required enormous quantities of human resources, such as scheduling, bed assignment, and patient flow optimization, are now being optimized through the assistance of AI.

Olive AI, for example, is a healthcare assistant that employs AI to automate routine administrative tasks and free hospital staff to focus on patient care.

AI-based scheduling systems ensure effective utilization of hospital resources, lowering patient waiting times and overall operational inefficiency. Automation at this level reduces the burden on healthcare professionals, who can then spend more time communicating with patients rather than paperwork and logistics.

AI is also revolutionizing genomic data analysis and precision medicine. AI can identify patient risks for many diseases by analyzing genetic markers and suggesting preventive action. *Tempus Labs* is leading the way with this innovation, employing AI to interpret genomic information and deliver tailored treatments based on a patient's genetic profile. This degree of accuracy enables physicians to make informed treatment decisions, enhancing patient outcomes and eliminating unnecessary procedures. AI-powered precision medicine is particularly critical in oncology, where a patient's genetic profile can significantly impact the success of targeted therapy.

The use of AI in medicine not only makes medicine more efficient; it's changing the face of medicine. From finding new medicines to the prevention of fraud, hospital administration, and targeted medicine, AI is creating a better, data-based healthcare system.

As AI progresses, its capability to improve medical research, maximize operations, and personalize treatments will grow, laying the groundwork for a future when healthcare is more accessible, more accurate, and more effective than ever.

The medical field benefits from artificial intelligence through diverse potential uses yet faces substantial obstacles before reaching total potential success. The major obstacle in AI-based medical decision-making appears through biased methods. The effectiveness of AI systems relies on their training data because any insufficient or non-diverse information could maintain existing healthcare inequalities. AI skin cancer diagnostic systems which receive most training from images of lighter complexions remain unable to detect conditions effectively in patients with darker complexions. Serious misdiagnoses can occur because of this situation which also worsens health inequities.

The construction of *unbiased AI systems* depends on developing diverse data sets that include all groups. Healthcare organizations along with AI developers should collaborate to obtain information from diverse demographic and socioeconomic groups to generate more fair AI applications.

Adequate testing of AI models across various population groups must be demonstrated before launching at scale. Healthcare professionals together with patients will build trust in AI when they clearly understand how AI processes make decisions.

Medical AI faces extensive obstacles within the compliance sector. The unprecedented pace of AI development exceeds the pace at which regulatory bodies are creating appropriate responses. AI applications enter clinical use since there exist no clearly defined validation and approval protocols making systems vulnerable to deficiencies in evaluation. The absence of proper regulation creates elevated risks of incorrect diagnoses which result in potential injuries to patients.

A standardized system for validating AI applications requires immediate development because healthcare institutions and patients demand it. The US Food and Drug Administration (USFDA) and European Medicines Agency (EMA) together with other regulatory bodies have initiated work on framework guidelines which must be applied during premarket evaluation of medical solutions powered by artificial intelligence for clinical use.

Another issue is the *ethical aspect of AI decision-making*. While human physicians can apply judgment and empathy, AI systems can only depend on data-driven algorithms. This creates concerns over accountability when AI produces errant or injurious decisions.

Who will be held accountable if an AI system diagnoses a patient? The hospital? The developer of the AI? The regulatory agency that cleared its use? Having clear legal and ethical frameworks on accountability will become crucial with the increasing adoption of AI.

Despite these difficulties, the future of AI in healthcare is extremely promising. Robotic surgery with the help of AI is already changing the medical world, enabling more accurate and less invasive procedures. These robotic devices, with AI algorithms at their helm, provide improved surgical precision and minimize the risk of human error.

Furthermore, AI-powered real-time monitoring systems for patients are increasingly becoming common, making it possible to detect deteriorating health conditions at an early stage and minimize hospital readmission rates.

One of the most promising developments in AI-based healthcare is the application of AI chatbots in mental health care. As the mental health disorder burden continues to grow, AI-based chatbots provide low-cost and affordable mental health care. Cognitive behaviour therapy-based chatbots, trained to address mental health disorders, offer instant assistance to patients suffering from depression, anxiety, and other mental illnesses.

Although they are not a replacement for human therapists, they are a necessary tool in filling the gap in mental health treatment.

AI is also revolutionizing pandemic readiness and disease forecasting. One such example is *BlueDot*, an AI system that accurately forecasted the spread of COVID-19 days ahead of conventional epidemiological models. Through the examination of international travel patterns, news articles, and health data, *BlueDot* was able to issue early alerts regarding the outbreak. Such predictive analytics powered by AI can be instrumental in detecting emerging health risks and facilitating swift response actions to contain outbreaks before they turn into global pandemics.

The effect of AI on healthcare affordability and accessibility cannot be overemphasized. AI-based solutions can lower the cost of healthcare by streamlining hospital operations, automating administrative processes, and enhancing diagnostic precision. This, in turn, makes quality healthcare more accessible and affordable, particularly in remote areas. *Telemedicine* platforms powered by AI are already transforming healthcare delivery by offering remote consultations, enabling patients to access medical advice without having to travel long distances.

But for AI to revolutionize healthcare, a balance must be achieved between innovation and ethical duty. Developers and medical professionals must collaborate to make sure that AI supports human decision-making instead of substituting it. Ethical deployment of AI demands ongoing oversight, transparency, and a focus on patient welfare. If deployed responsibly, AI can fill healthcare gaps and build a more efficient, patient-focused medical system.

As AI develops further, it is evident that its application in healthcare will only grow. The success of integration depends on the elimination of biases, the creation of strong regulatory systems, and the preservation of a human-centric focus. The future of AI in healthcare is not merely about technological progress, it is about developing a system where technology complements human knowledge to provide improved health outcomes for everyone. By embracing AI's potential while navigating its challenges, the world can move towards a future where high-quality, personalized healthcare is accessible to everyone, regardless of their location or socioeconomic status.

AI is not just revolutionizing mental health treatment but also advancing population health, aged care, and patient recovery through new startups.

Singapore-based Govin Capital has been leading the way in investing in AI-based healthcare solutions that cater to various needs. For example, *Aktivolabs* in Singapore uses AI to improve population health and longevity, supporting preventive healthcare practices. Another Singapore-based investee company, *Kinexcs*, specializes in patient rehabilitation after Total Knee Replacement (TKR) procedures, employing AI-powered rehabilitation devices to enhance results. Another significant investment is *eBeecare*, which offers AI-powered homecare services for the elderly, providing quality nursing care customized to individual requirements. Aside from elderly and rehabilitation nursing, AI is also serving a vital function in distant health monitoring. *RayIOT*, based in the US and India, has created non-contact, non-invasive AI-driven breath monitoring technology to monitor neonatal and elderly respiratory well-being. In contrast, *Kare4U Healthcare* is changing the insurance industry by opening healthcare access through blockchain and AI-driven real-time health insurance solutions, enhancing transparency and accessibility in healthcare.

Moreover, AI is revolutionizing women's health, especially in reproductive care and fertility management.

Platforms driven by AI help predict ovulation cycles, evaluate fertility potential, and offer personalized advice for those in need of conception support. These technologies not only provide personalized reproductive health information but also assist in mass education, creating inclusivity and dispelling stigmas about women's health. AI-powered chatbots and digital assistants also guarantee women 24/7 access to credible reproductive health information so that they can make well-informed decisions. With further development of AI, its influence on mental wellbeing, geriatric care, rehabilitation, and female health will only continue to grow, setting the stage for a more inclusive, predictive, patient-focused healthcare system.

Chapter 11: Govin Entrepreneurship Management (GEM) Leadership Insights

Goran S Malm

Former President, Asia Pacific, Dell Computer Corporation

Former President, GE Asia-Pacific & GE Medical Asia, Singapore

Chairman & Board Director, Govin Capital, Singapore

Mr Malm held senior executive roles in Dell Computer and GE Medical Systems. From November 1999 to November 2000, Mr Malm served as President, Asia Pacific and Senior Vice President of Dell Computer Corporation, being responsible for Dell's business operations in the region, with $3 billion sales revenue and 3500 employees, and a growth rate of 50% yearly. With a base in Singapore, he held executive responsibility for Dell's operations and expansive distribution network in all markets across Asia Pacific, serving customers in 48 countries. In addition, he also had responsibility for Dell's materials management and two manufacturing facilities in the region: The Asia Pacific Customer Center in Penang, Malaysia, and the China Customer Center in Xiamen, China. Main sponsor of Dell's establishment in India and the Dell Ventures' investments in Asia – 7 deals completed with more than $60 million invested.

Prior to Dell, Mr Goran Malm served as Senior Vice President-General Electric Company and President of General Electric Asia-Pacific from October 1997 to November 1999. As one of 20 Senior Vice Presidents of General Electric with a base in Hong Kong and with direct reporting line to the Chairman John F. Welch of the General Electric Company, responsible for the Asia-Pacific region, embracing all GE's eleven businesses, including GE Capital, plus the national executive organizations in all major countries. The Asian businesses consisted of 93 legal units in 14 countries (2/3 of them joint ventures) with 45,000 employees. The accumulated sales revenue reached $10 billion in '99 (growing +1% in '98 and +30% in '99). Earnings grew by double digits both '98 (+19%) and '99 (+22%). Major SVP initiatives during the Asia crisis were Risk Management (Receivable and currency exposures), Sourcing (up 50% in '99 to $1.4 billion from emerging Asia), Business Development (60 deals concluded – 50% GE Capital – 50% GE Industrial) plus People Development (localization) forming a strong basis for future business growth.

Mr Malm served as President & CEO, GE Medical Systems Asia, from January 1992 to September 1997

As one of the top 30 Vice Presidents of General Electric with a base in Tokyo, responsible for all Asian business activities within GE Medical Systems. Managed to grow external sales from US$384 million in 1991 to US$968 million by 1997 and improve the net income from $12 million to $71 million during the same period. GEMS Asia employed by Sep.'97 3,450 people in sales and marketing, service, product development, production, and sourcing.

The main strategic approach was to win locally and become an insider in several Asian markets early. To achieve the growth objectives, a shareholding majority was acquired in two existing joint ventures (Wipro-GE and Samsung GE), seven new joint ventures were formed with GE majority shareholding (GE-Elpro and GE BEL in India, GE Haiying and GE Haulun in China, GE Hospitech in Thailand, GE Mediland in Taiwan, and GETI in Indonesia,) and one Japanese acquisition was realized (GE Tanaka).

GEMS-Asia developed and manufactured more than 50% of all equipment sold in Asia (MR, CT, X-Ray, and Ultrasound) and had about $210 million in exports to the Americas and Europe.

Mr Malm's Key Message to Biomedical Entrepreneurs

1. Outline a winning and exciting vision for the organisation
2. Deliver Operating Commitments by Being Ahead Of The Game (Cost Down Before Price Down)

3. Continuously Improve the Organization's Competency by Recruitment, Training, Rewards and Career Planning
4. Act As Strong Role Model for Integrity And Boundaryless Behaviour Inside and Outside the Company

GEMSA Executive Staff Meeting in May 1995, Hawaii

D A Prasanna

Former CEO & MD, Wipro GE, India

Board Director, Govin Capital, Singapore

Author, Innovate Locally to Win Globally

https://amzn.eu/d/deUcM74

Q1: What drew you to medical technology and Key highlights under your leadership at Wipro, Manipal?

When GE and Wipro invited me to be the first CEO and MD of WiproGE Medical Systems, mandate was 'grow GE from #7 to No 1or 2 in 5 years ETHICALLY'. In a medical technology market, where 80% of transactions involved over invoicing, under invoicing, commission to recommending doctors, speed money to get import license for customer in Delhi, industry leaders and key customers advised that unless you are' commercially flexible' GE will not get more than 5% market share. Neither GE nor Wipro had any answers on way forward. It had to be figured out by CEO and his team. I looked back at Wipro Infotech - a computer business built by my colleagues Narasimhan and Soota. They had found a way. So I took the plunge to find a way.

Q2: What were some of the toughest challenges that stood in your way during your tenure at Wipro & Manipal and how did you cope with them?

In WiproGE, we soon realized that in a urban market, competition was entrenched and had set the rules of engagement with customers. With those rules we could not become a leader, and every win was with a modest margin. We realized that we have to create a market, where we can set the rules of the game. We focused on semi urban cities (known in India as tier 2 cities), where successful medical practitioners and entrepreneurs, aspired to setup smaller hospitals and diagnostic centers. WiproGE teamed with them and overcame every constraint to make it a financially viable investment. We could set the rules of customer engagement and created a new market and took majority share. Primary reason for viability was a scan affordable by a semiurban patient and the convenience of local access. This drove our goals of local manufacture. Create a diagnostic center at half the investment of competitors, at double the speed. Once we were successful in Indian market, we wanted to be at the decision making table in GE Healthcare. This was not possible for a $10M revenue business in a $3B co. so we set a goal to become a $200M business and got there in seven years. $100M in local market and $100M in exports. We had to aspire big and overcome every hurdle and create market.

In Manipal, a 50 year old institution, the key goal was to corporatize. First task was to evolve with Founders a fix, sell or close strategy for non core business. Dr. Ranjan Pai was very smart in monetizing for best value, building a corpus in the family office. Second step was to instill a mindset that 'not for profit' healthcare and education institutions can sustain only if the operations produce an economic surplus. From a satisfactory under performer, the group was transformed into a high performing organization through benchmarking, target orientation and cultural change.

Q3: What advice would you give to young entrepreneurs in medical technology?

Medical technology adoption by a hospital does not happen just because your product is clinically superior or offers reduction in procedure cost. A doctor is held to revenue target in the hospital. If your product reduces patient charge by 50%, he has to do double to procedures to earn same revenue. He wont' adopt. Hospital owner is trying to move up the value chain. He is fine to buy fancy technology which positions the hospital as moving up the value chain. And he will refuse a product which medical community thinks as cheap. If insurance company does not qualify your new procedure, the market will not buy. This reality has to be fully understood by MedTech entrepreneur for scaling the revenue.

Q4: How do you see the future of biomedical industry growth in India?

Bright.

Growth of market for healthcare is driven by affordability of technology and ability of patients to access it. Growth Capital is NOT in short supply for healthcare services to grow deeper into India, so there is a push from service providers. Pull from patients is driven by ACCESS. Physical access of medical facilities has increased due to push. Lack of doctors and specialists is overcome with remote service through telemedicine. Financial access has increased by the central govt scheme of Ayushman Bharat providing 5lacs per year per family supplemented in many states by state schemes. Digital access is essential to access ayushman like schemes. Smartphones - inexpensive is in every Indian hand. Making it feasible. A combination of affordable technology, access and capital has created condition for exponential growth of sector. The MedTech manufacturing ecosystem has also grown making Indian MedTech accepted globally. There is no better time than now to be part of this growth momentum.

Q5. Importance of mentorship for startups- do you see startups that were mentored fare better than those that don't?

Mentoring is one factor, but not the most important. Factors for success of entrepreneurs, find a real unmet need, be passionate to make your idea succeed, early-stage risk fund with non-dilutive grant, have skin in the game with staking personal money beyond sweat equity. Employ one or two seasoned executives to lead with you.

C P Bothra

Chairman, Lyrus Life Sciences, India

Former, Founder & Managing Director, Medreich, India

1. What was the reason to start Medreich and how did it evolve over time?

Medreich was established in Bangalore, Karnataka, India—at a time when the city was still emerging as an industrial hub and housed only five pharmaceutical manufacturing facilities. The decision to locate the company in Bangalore was strategic. The climate was ideal for pharmaceutical operations, and Karnataka boasted nearly 50% of India's pharmacy colleges, creating a rich talent pool. The rise of the IT and technology sectors in the region further inspired our vision, creating a stimulating ecosystem of innovation and efficiency.

From these modest beginnings, Medreich grew steadily and purposefully. Our philosophy was simple yet powerful: work exclusively with multinational companies and deliver uncompromising quality. This strategy not only differentiated us in the marketplace but also instilled deep trust among our partners. There was no dilution of quality at any stage, and this commitment became the cornerstone of our growth. As we consistently delivered on our promises, our client base expanded, our credibility grew, and so did the size and scale of our operations.

2. What are you especially proud of during your leadership at Medreich?

Among all the milestones, what fills me with the greatest pride is the team we built. From just three people at inception, we scaled up to a thriving workforce of over 3,200 employees. But beyond the numbers, what stands out is the culture we nurtured. We introduced a "buddy scheme" that empowered every individual to rise, learn, and lead. This inclusive growth model ensured that ownership was not concentrated—it was shared. We believed in creating leaders, not just employees.

That culture of empowerment translated into results. Our teams consistently outperformed industry benchmarks, driven by a sense of purpose and belonging. Medreich also adopted a bold internal target of achieving 100% on-time delivery—an aspiration few dared to articulate. We came remarkably close, with a delivery success rate exceeding 98%, and this relentless pursuit of operational excellence became a defining trait of our brand.

3. Can you share your experience about the JV with Substipharm and how it helped grow Medreich?

Substipharm, a highly regarded French pharmaceutical company with a global footprint, became a valued partner at a crucial stage in our journey. Known for their rigorous standards and exacting expectations, they exemplified what it meant to pursue perfection. After evaluating several formulation development partners worldwide, they found in Medreich a company that met their benchmark—and more.

Their decision to take equity in Medreich validated our capabilities on a global scale. The partnership brought not just capital, but also a new level of sophistication to our systems and processes. When we eventually decided to sell the company, we approached Substipharm to exit their stake. They did so gracefully, underscoring the deep mutual respect between both parties. Ours was the only Indian company at the time with a French strategic partner, and this uniqueness helped shape Medreich's identity in the international pharmaceutical landscape.

4. What are the biggest challenges facing the Indian Pharma industry?

The Indian pharmaceutical industry, despite its immense potential and global standing, faces a fundamental challenge: internal competition. There's a pervasive belief that offering the lowest price is the surest path to success. But this is a misjudgment. Competing solely on price erodes value and often compromises quality—a dangerous trade-off in healthcare.

What truly sets companies apart is their ability to deliver consistent quality on time. This, and only this, should be the mantra for Indian pharma companies aspiring to lead globally. India has the talent, the infrastructure, and the demand. The industry must now shift its focus from cost-cutting to quality-building. Growth is not a zero-sum game. There is room for everyone to flourish—provided the commitment to quality is non-negotiable.

5. How did you plan the exit strategy for Medreich? Please share your strategies, key learnings, and takeaways for other smaller pharma companies.

Our initial intent was never to sell Medreich in its entirety. We were exploring partial divestment to bring in a strategic partner. Then came Perrigo, USA with an attractive offer. Financially, it was compelling—but ethically, it posed challenges. Their vision involved automating operations and exiting a large part of the workforce. We couldn't, in good conscience, support such a transition.

Then came Meiji Seika Pharma Co., Ltd., a Japanese company with a wholly different perspective. They valued continuity. Their proposal preserved the Medreich name, upheld our business strategy, and—most importantly—committed to retaining every employee for a minimum of five years. This resonated with our values. Despite the lower financial valuation, we chose Meiji because it aligned with our long-term view: people matter more than price.

Key Learnings: Over the years, we discovered that success—especially in a global business with presence in 92 countries—boils down to two simple principles: deliver high quality and deliver it on time. This became our competitive advantage. For smaller pharma companies, I would say this—never compromise on these two pillars. Everything else will follow. Medreich's journey is proof that purpose-driven growth, built on integrity and consistency, always finds its place on the global stage.

Gourab Mukherjee

Co-Founder & CEO

Aktivo Labs.

Q1: How did you come up with the idea of Aktivolabs, and what was the most challenging part for you to get it off the ground?

The idea for Aktivolabs came from a very personal place. Over the years, I watched close friends and family members — seemingly healthy individuals — fall seriously ill because early warning signs were missed. It made me realize how reactive our healthcare systems are: we often wait for disease to strike before taking action.

I became obsessed with the idea that prevention had to be proactive — and that technology, used wisely, could make early intervention simple and scalable. Starting Aktivolabs was exhilarating but challenging. The hardest part wasn't just building the platform — it was building trust. We were asking insurers, employers, and healthcare providers to believe that simple lifestyle data, captured passively through smartphones and wearables, could predict future health risks. Earning their confidence required scientific rigor, partnerships with top academic institutions, and an unshakable commitment to our mission.

Q2: What's your vision for the future of digital health, and how can Aktivolabs contribute to it?

Our journey has shaped a clear vision for the future: digital health will become invisible, personal, and predictive — seamlessly woven into our daily lives, quietly nudging us toward better health.

The true game-changer will be AI. Artificial intelligence will allow us to detect risks earlier, personalize interventions more intelligently, and reach millions of people with tailored guidance — long before diseases develop.

At Aktivolabs, AI is at the core of our platform. By turning passive behavioral data — such as movement, sleep, and habits — into predictive health scores, we empower individuals and organizations to make smarter decisions today that safeguard health tomorrow. I truly believe that soon, knowing your "Aktivo Score" will be as common — and as vital — as knowing your blood pressure or cholesterol levels. But unlike traditional measures, it won't just describe your current health; it will predict your future well-being.

Q3: Can you narrate a success story of how Aktivolabs has helped a patient's life positively and the impact that Aktivolabs has generated to date?

One story that stays with me is about a young father working at a company that adopted Aktivolabs as part of their wellness program. Though he felt healthy, our platform flagged hidden metabolic risks through his Aktivo Score. Motivated by the early warning, he made small but consistent changes — walking daily, improving sleep habits — and six months later, reversed early signs of pre-diabetes he hadn't even known he had. Stories like his remind us why we do what we do.

Today, Aktivolabs has impacted over half a million lives across Asia, the Middle East, and beyond — helping individuals take charge of their health journeys and enabling insurers and employers to shift from treating illness to preventing it. We believe in a world where no one should lose their health silently — and where prevention, powered by AI and human insight, becomes second nature for everyone.

Patti White & Peter Galen

Hemex Health

Transforming Diagnostics, Empowering Lives

At Hemex Health, our vision was born from a deeply rooted belief: millions of people—particularly women and children in low-income regions—deserve access to accurate, timely healthcare diagnostics. Yet, in many parts of the world, a simple blood test can be the difference between life and death—and for too many, even that is out of reach. Founded in 2016, we set out to bridge that gap through innovative, affordable, and accessible point-of-care technologies.

One of our greatest challenges was to create a diagnostic solution that delivered both world-class performance and affordability. The reality is, gold-standard diagnostics are often expensive, complicated, and require infrastructure not available in remote or underserved areas. Overcoming this challenge led to the development of Gazelle™, our compact, battery-powered diagnostic platform. Built using miniaturized electrophoresis technology, Gazelle delivers lab-quality results from a single drop of blood and is designed for ease of use in low-resource settings.

Our work is especially impactful for children's and women's health. Sickle cell and related disorders kills around 1,000 children every day with most dying undiagnosed. For a few pennies a day 70-80% of these children can be saved.

Severe anaemia, often caused by iron deficiency or genetic disorders like sickle cell disease and beta thalassemia, remains a leading cause of maternal mortality. Our hemoglobinopathy and ferritin tests are helping frontline health workers detect these conditions early—before they lead to complications. In this way, we are helping to protect both mothers and their unborn children, bringing critical care closer to home.

A breakthrough moment for us was being included in India's National Sickle Cell Elimination Program. This milestone validated our approach and accelerated our impact. Today, over 870 Gazelle devices are being used in Primary and Community Health Centers across Odisha, Tamil Nadu, and Gujarat. In one moving example, a young tribal woman in Odisha was diagnosed with severe anemia during pregnancy thanks to Gazelle. Because of early detection, she received treatment that likely saved her life and the life of her child. These are the moments that remind us why our work matters.

We see the future of healthcare as one where equity drives innovation. Technology alone is not enough—it must be accessible and adapted to the real needs of communities. Gazelle's over-the-air upgrade capabilities allow it to evolve with new diagnostic capabilities, and its digital integration reduces transcription errors and enables efficient health data tracking. These features make it a future-ready solution for global health challenges.

The India-U.S. partnership has been critical to our success. As a company headquartered in Portland, Oregon with a strong and growing presence in India, we've had the opportunity to benefit from the strengths of both ecosystems. Collaborations with the India Health Fund, SAMRIDH, Novartis, and the CDC have helped us scale operations to over 1,500 sites across many Indian states, with an ambitious goal to test millions of individuals—many in remote, tribal communities. These collaborations exemplify how global partnerships can drive local impact.

Looking ahead, we believe the two biggest transformations needed in the next decade are diagnostic accessibility and affordability. Too many people still suffer and die due to lack of timely testing. We are committed to being part of the solution, continuing to develop technologies that deliver high-quality diagnostics where they're needed most.

Our greatest strength as a team has been staying laser-focused on our mission—developing products that deliver gold-standard performance at a price point that enables wide adoption. We constantly challenge ourselves to meet the demands of both users and the market without compromising our values.

To the next generation of innovators—especially young women—we offer this: build a strong foundation in science and technology, learn the business of healthcare, sharpen your communication skills, and surround yourselves with mentors and supporters. Resilience and community will carry you far. And as you succeed, we hope you will lift others with you.

At Hemex Health, we believe that a single drop of blood can change life. Through passion, partnership, and purpose, we're working to build a world where everyone has access to the diagnostic tools they need to thrive. Our journey continues—and we're proud to be part of a global movement transforming healthcare for all.

Index

Photos:

Photos: Dr G P Sastry, Father and Mrs G Sakuntala, Mother who motivated the author to pursue a career in Biotechnology and instilled principles of financial as well as risk management

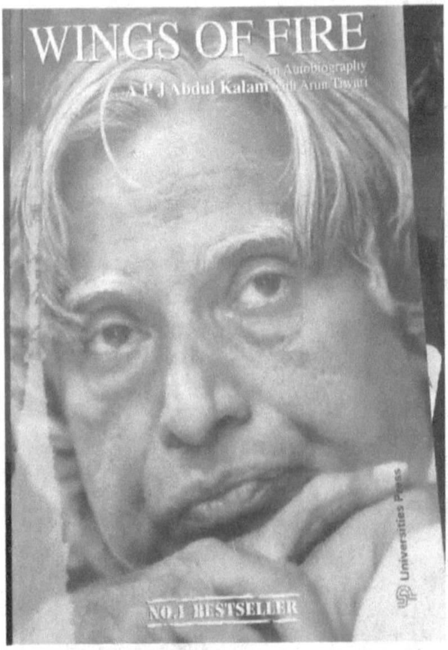

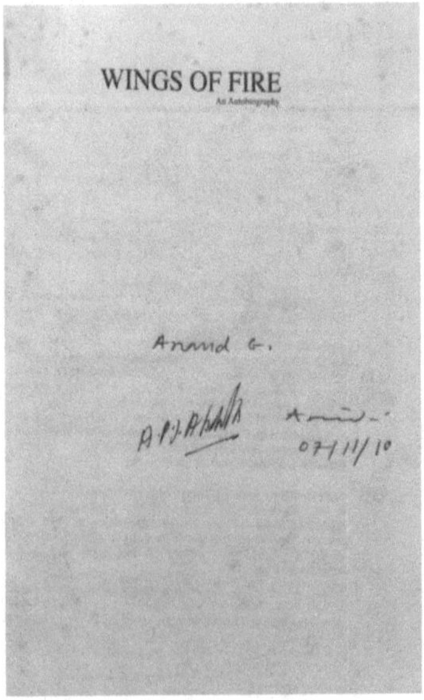

Photos: Autograph from Dr A P J Abdul Kalam, during his visit to Singapore, 2010

P

Photo: Dr A P J Abdul Kalam Award for Promoting Innovation & Entrepreneurship from Shri Ram Naik, Former Governor of Uttar Pradesh & Minister of Petroleum & Natural Gas of India,2017

Photos: INSEAD Singapore, 2025

Photo: ESCP School of Business, London campus

Photo: EMBA students from ESCP School of Business, France & ESA Business School, Beirut

Photo: Dr Anand with Prof Francesco Venuti, Dean of Executive MBA & General Management Programme, ESCP France & Academic Director Executive MBA, ESA Business School, Beirut & Prof Frederic Jallat, Professor at ESCP Business School, France

Verses Kindler Publication

Verses Kindler Publication

Reach us through our website -

https://www.verseskindlerpublication.com/

For more information visit our

Instagram or Facebook page.

www.ingramcontent.com/pod-product-compliance
Lightning Source LLC
Chambersburg PA
CBHW061811230926
51852CB00003B/88
* 9 7 8 9 3 4 9 5 3 2 1 1 3 *